War Moments

Images & Stories of Combat in Iraq, Afghanistan & Beyond

With foreword by R.M. Schneiderman,
former deputy editor of Newsweek

Text & Photographs by
Ed Darack

Amherst Media, Inc. Buffalo, NY

War Moments is dedicated to all members of the United States Armed Services, past, present, and future. Notably, I'd like to highlight members of the Marine Corps units with whom I've embedded in combat in Afghanistan and Iraq, as well as in the United States and abroad, during training operations.

Published by:
Amherst Media, Inc., P.O. Box 538, Buffalo, N.Y. 14213
www.AmherstMedia.com

Publisher: Craig Alesse
Associate Publisher: Katie Kiss
Senior Editor/Production Manager: Michelle Perkins
Editors: Barbara A. Lynch-Johnt, Beth Alesse
Acquisitions Editor: Harvey Goldstein
Editorial Assistance from: Ray Bakos, Carey Miller, Rebecca Rudell, Jen Sexton-Riley
Business Manager: Sarah Loder
Marketing Associate: Tonya Flickinger

ISBN-13: 978-1-68203-394-4
Library of Congress Control Number: 2018960373
Printed in The United States of America.
10 9 8 7 6 5 4 3 2 1

Contents

About the Author

Ed Darack has covered America's modern wars as both a writer and as a photographer for more than a decade. He's embedded with combat troops in the most dangerous, austere throes of war a total of six times—twice in Iraq and four times in Afghanistan. He's also embedded dozens of times with the U.S. military during training exercises, both at home and overseas.

Always working independently, Darack has produced a tremendous volume of military themed imagery. Tens of millions of people have seen his photographs on the covers and interiors of books, newspapers, magazines, and via online venues across the globe. His war and military imagery credits include: the cover of *Newsweek*, the cover of a *Time* magazine special edition, the cover of a #2 *New York Times* bestseller on Pat Tillman, the cover of Germany's *Stern* magazine, two covers of Smithsonian's *Air & Space* magazine, the covers of a host of military themed books, *The New York Times*, and *Vanity Fair*, among many other venues.

He's the author of a number of books on modern military topics, including *Victory Point* (Penguin, 2009), and *The Final Mission of Extortion 17* (Smithsonian Books, 2017). Darack is a contributing editor to Smithsonian's *Air & Space* magazine, where he writes frequently about military aviation topics. Other military writing credits of his include *Newsweek, Foreign Policy, The Marine Corps Gazette, Proceedings of the U.S. Naval Institute*, and *Leatherneck* magazine.

For more information, please visit:

www.darack.com
www.facebook.com/ed.darack1
www.instagram.com/eddarack
www.twitter.com/eddarack

LICENSING AND PRINTS:

Ed Darack's images are available for licensing through Ed Darack Photography as well as through a number of the world's leading agencies, including Superstock and Getty Images. For information on purchasing archival prints of his work, visit www.darack.com.

Foreword

R.M. Schneiderman,
former deputy editor,
Newsweek magazine

A makeshift parking lot for tanks and a SAW gunner silhouetted by the sun. Afghan children strolling through the shadows, and a Beanie Baby attached to an air drop. These are some of the images Ed Darack captures in his powerful new book *War Moments*, a collection of combat photography from the deadly conflicts in Iraq and Afghanistan.

Today, more than fifteen years after these wars began, Americans seem to have forgotten about them. Darack's photographs, however, are not so easily erased from our memories. They stay with us, sometimes because they are disturbing—a man holding the component wire of an IED—and other times because they are shockingly normal—Marines sleeping in the sun or devouring MREs (meal ready to eat).

What ties these images together is their portrait of humanity. They don't gloss over the tragic, frightening mess of war. But they do manage to honor the men and women involved—Afghans, Americans, Iraqis. Seeing their faces, watching them in action or in repose, we cannot push them out of our minds. Ed Darack's photographs are indelible.

Introduction

"Remember to keep your head down when they start shooting at you!" U.S. Army Staff Sergeant Rick Scavetta yelled over the din of two screaming turboshaft engines and the THWACK-THWACK-THWACK of spinning rotor blades. Under the press of more than one hundred pounds of gear, including five cameras and hundreds of rolls of film, I walked underneath those spinning rotors and through the hot, pungent exhaust of those turboshaft engines. A few more steps brought me to the base of the loading ramp of the helicopter to which those engines and rotor blades belonged, a burly U.S. Army CH-47D Chinook, call sign "Big Windy 21." The tandem-rotor aircraft idled on the south side of Bagram Airfield, America's largest base in Afghanistan during Operation Enduring Freedom, the official name of the United States' War in Afghanistan from 2001 to 2014. I turned to see Rick, the public affairs officer assigned to coordinate my combat embed, laughing and giving a downward motion with both hands as he mouthed "keep your head down!!" I smiled nervously, then climbed into the Chinook. Wrestling my gear up that ramp marked the true beginning—the point of no return—of an odyssey into a completely unknown world to me at that point in my life: war. That first combat embed for me began in late September of 2005, when the wars in Afghanistan and Iraq raged at full force. I had come to Afghanistan alone, as an independent photographer and writer, without any formal training, and without any umbrella organization above me to provide guidance or support. "Affiliati on: Freelance" was emblazoned on my official media identification badge. Six months earlier I had spent two weeks at the Marine Corps Mountain Warfare Training Center, and during that time, embedded with the 2nd Battalion of the 3rd Marine Regiment during their pre-deployment training for Afghanistan. The battalion invited me to join them for their deployment at the end of that two weeks. I accepted, and my life changed forever.

I had already been a photographer for more than fifteen years at that point. The subjects I shot included outdoor, landscape, weather, travel, and adventure sports. Jumping into an active combat zone—the battalion sent me to one of the most dangerous extremities of the war in Afghanistan, the eastern Kunar Province—proved to be an incredible "learning and development by fire" experience. I took all that I'd gleaned from my previous photography work and applied it to creating images of war. I quickly developed my own style, one based as much in aesthetic appeal as in the spirit of classic photojournalism. With each composition, I sought to graphically and artfully convey the most salient moments I experienced and witnessed while embedded with U.S. forces. And I experienced and witnessed much: profound bravery and strength, unwavering dedication and boldness, humor and raucous laughter. I witnessed incredible natural beauty and unknown cultures juxtaposed against the realities of modern war. And I experienced spasms of anticipation and anxiety, some anger, and on my part, moments of intense fear. To photographically convey these diverse moments of war, I hyper-concentrated on each composition, maintaining an eye for graphical flow, balance, texture, and powerful admixtures of color and contrast. After that first embed, I was hooked. I wanted to experience more, to learn more, to document more—to photographically capture more of the most riveting, intense, surprising, confounding, ironic, and even beautiful moments of humanity at its most extreme, those of war.

The artistic pursuit proved to be a dynamic, multivariate evolution, the most powerful and compelling component of which being the relationships forged with the troops themselves as I followed them into some of the most dangerous places in the world. A Marine asked me with a smile as I boarded a helicopter at the start of my first ever combat operation, "You ready to take pictures of us as we walk through the valley of the shadow of death?" I undertook six total combat embeds, four times to Afghanistan and twice to Iraq—all as an independent—and I forged many great friendships in the process. I eventually would experience the agony of losing some of those friends, all of them far too young.

War Moments is a dream project for me, for many reasons. The book represents a culmination of years of toil, risk, planning, and then very careful editing. It's a very personal project, one that has stirred vivid memories and some intense emotions as I've put it together. I've assembled a complimentary set of some of my all-time favorite war images for the book out of hundreds of thousands that I created over the years. These include images made during my combat embeds in Iraq and in Afghanistan, as well as during the dozens of training exercises that I covered. Subjects include personnel and assets of all four U.S. military service branches and the National Guard, as well as some images of foreign ally combatants and locals.

There are no traditional sections to *War Moments*; rather, each image and its associated caption stands as its own "chapter." I used an admixture of criteria in both deciding which images to include in the book, and how to order them. These criteria included: image subject(s), location, and graphical components of the image itself. I spent a great deal of time and thought writing each caption to tell what I felt to be the most appropriate story behind each image—all of these photographs have at least a few, if not many, stories behind them, so this proved a difficult but very important task. Some captions explain technical details of an image's subject, some focus on how I created a photograph, some feature personal insight of a moment, and some—the most important to me—serve as a memorial to those lost.

My overarching intent of this book is to provide a unique and lucid window onto modern war and the modern war fighter. I want readers to immerse themselves in each image, and to understand each photographically captured moment through its narrative. The format of War Moments allows readers to start anywhere in the book, to read it cover to cover, or to jump around—it's a visual odyssey, one that will bring a greater depth and breadth of understanding with each turned page.

——Ed Darack
Fort Collins, Colorado

SAW Gunner

Hindu Kush of eastern Afghanistan's Kunar Province

The Marine in this photograph, who is mostly silhouetted by the rising morning sun, is Jeremy Sandvick Monroe. Nineteen at the time, he was a SAW (Squad Automatic Weapon) gunner, one of the most difficult and important jobs in Marine Corps infantry. Jeremy was taking part in Operation Valdez, launched to locate a cave used by the Taliban and Al Qaeda to hide a mortar system they employed to attack Firebase Blessing. The home to Jeremy and other Marines during their deployment, the frequently-assaulted base was named after a member of the 75th Ranger Regiment, Jay Blessing, who was killed in the area in 2003. A mortar volley just a few days prior to this image killed twenty-year-old Marine Steven Valdez, a member of Jeremy's platoon. The Marines eventually found the cave, and promptly destroyed it with 150 pounds of C-4 high explosive.

I shot this image of Jeremy with a Nikon F6 film camera with a 70–200 f/2.8 lens on Fujichrome Velvia Film (ISO 50) during the morning patrol. As Jeremy and other Marines ascended a hillside, I ran up in front of them and then off to the side to find an ideal spot, then composed a vertical image and shot a series of images. This was the best, and one that I shared with Jeremy the following year during his training for his battalion's upcoming deployment to Iraq.

Jeremy was killed in Iraq shortly after that training, in early October of 2006. He was twenty years old.

Expending Flares

Over the Anbar Province of Iraq

In May of 2007 I was embedded with the 2nd Marine Air Wing (Forward), based out of Al Asad Airbase in western Iraq's Al Anbar Province. The deployed air wing consisted of a number of Marine Corps aircraft squadrons, including Marine Heavy Helicopter Squadron 362, or HMH-362. Known as the "Ugly Angels," HMH-362 flew the venerable Sikorsky CH-53D "Sea Stallion" heavy lift helicopter, transporting troops, food, weapons, ammunition, spare parts—just about anything—throughout western Iraq. These flights were always dangerous, for a number of reasons, from potential malfunctions to enemy fire. Most notable among these threats, however was that posed by heat-seeking anti-aircraft missiles. Countering this threat, Sea Stallions and other American military helicopters can expend flares, which confuse inbound missiles with their own heat signatures.

I photographed this Sea Stallion testing its flare system just after lifting off on a re-supply mission. I used a Nikon D200 fitted with a 70–200 f/2.8 zoom lens, and carefully coordinated with the pilots both Sea Stallions to get just the right angle and distance for the shot.

Resupply Drop

Sky above Hindu Kush of eastern Afghanistan's Kunar Province

One of the most important components of running a war is logistics—in a nutshell, getting all types of supplies to the troops—whether those troops are in a large forward operating base, or far, far away from those big, sprawling facilities, in territory often surrounded by the enemy. For the latter, air resupply drops, formally called Container Delivery System drops (CDS), bring welcome food, water, ammunition, and other necessities. During a combat operation deep in the Hindu Kush of eastern Afghanistan, near the border with Pakistan, supplies were running low for a platoon of Marines of the 2nd Battalion of the 3rd Marine Regiment with whom I was embedded in October of 2005. A low hum announced the approach of an Air Force

C-130E Hercules cargo airplane one late afternoon, quickly followed by a roar of the aircraft's four turboprop engines as it passed overhead. Six pallets stacked with supplies *(above)* sailed out the rear of the Hercules attached to parachutes. As the C-130 sped into the sunset, the supplies quietly drifted toward the waiting Marines, who very eagerly tore into the rations once on the ground.

I photographed this image with a Nikon F6 film camera with a 70–200mm f/2.8 zoom lens using Fujichrome Velvia (ISO 50) film.

Christmas in Afghanistan

Hindu Kush of eastern Afghanistan's Kunar Province

Despite the importance and seriousness of providing resupply drops to troops far away from forward operating bases like the one pictured on the facing page, those who package these supplies understand the importance of some humor and levity. After that Air Force supply drop landed, and the Marines converged, their eyes locked immediately onto some colorful "passengers" the Air Force personnel had attached: Beanie Babies. At the time of the drop I was tagging along with Marine rifleman Charles Christmas *(facing page)*, who posed for the image "Christmas in Afghanistan" as he showed off one of the colorful bears.

I shot this image with a Nikon F6 film camera with a 17–35mm f/2.8 wide angle zoom on Fujichrome Velvia (ISO 50) film. I used a Nikon Speedlight for fill lighting.

Dusk Patrol

Albu Hyatt, Al Anbar Province of Iraq

I spent nearly two months on the ground with a battalion of U.S. Marines in the Al Anbar Province of western Iraq in early 2007. Those weeks proved to be some of the most difficult, exhausting, and at (many) times absolutely terrifying of my life. Over ten years later, I still find myself sweating and clenching my fists at some of the memories. No place was safe, no time was safe. Al Qaeda in Iraq (AQI) had killed more than twenty members of the battalion by the time I had arrived. They killed with sniper attacks, ambushes, mortar attacks, and perhaps most insidiously, they killed with improvised explosive device (IED) attacks—bombs hidden under roads, trails, and even in mud walls.

Just after arriving at the battalion's headquarters, Lieutenant Regan Turner grabbed me and pulled me into a patrol. Ever on the lookout for any form of enemy activity, the Marines were particularly focused on finding hidden IEDs. When we came to a *wadi* (dry stream bed), I sprinted down into it as a Marine *(top)* continued along the bridge that spanned the wadi, searching for any signs of IEDs. Heart pounding as I moved across the sun-scorched earth, I composed shot after shot of him silhouetted by dusk light. I don't remember what camera or lens I used, but the image was shot on Fujichrome Velvia (ISO 100).

Nighttime Insert

Alpena Combat Readiness Training Center, Michigan

One of my first embeds came in 2004. I covered some training of members of a Special Operations Weather Team in Michigan. Special Operations Weather Teams help plan and sometimes execute special operations missions through their expertise and input in meteorology. Special Operations Weather Teams, or SOWTs, have proven vital in the country's recent conflicts for both land, sea, and air units—often weather proves to be the most potent enemy. SOWTs are often

tasked with inserting, via parachute, into combat zones.

To photograph this member during training for a night-time insert *(right)*, I used a Nikon F5 with a 50mm f/1.4 lens, and held it up to a night vision monocle.

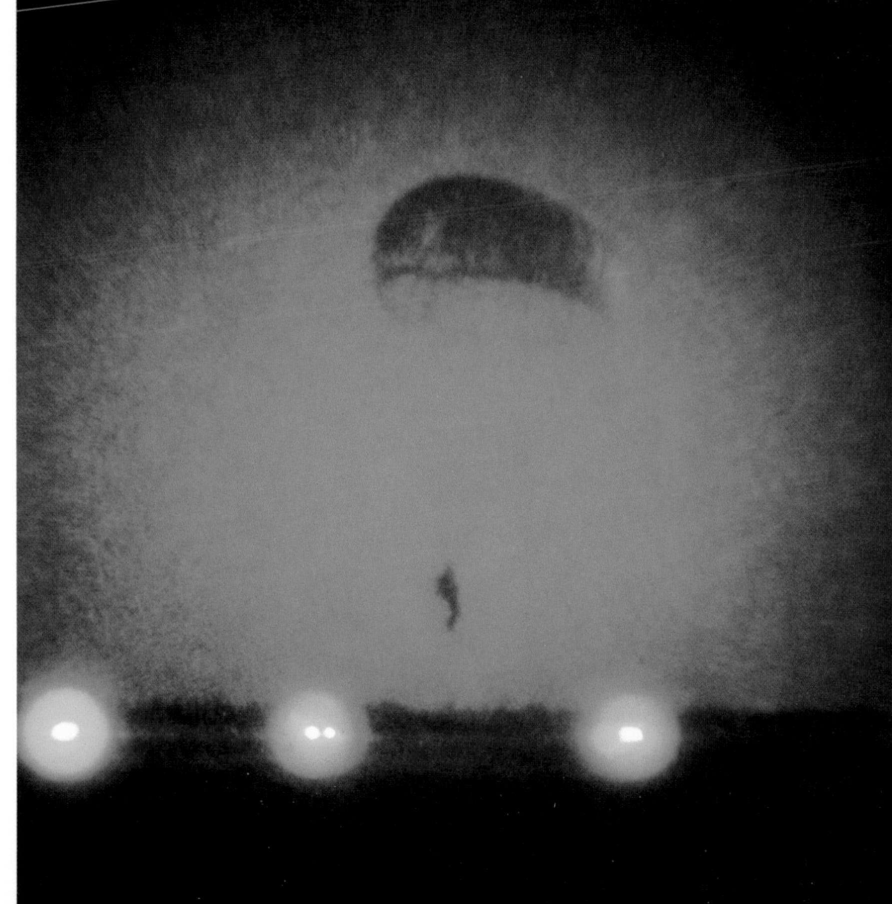

Chow

Forward Operating Base Marjah, Helmand Province, Afghanistan

Food, colloquially known as *chow* throughout the U.S. military, is incredibly important to the war fighter. Good, hot chow is especially coveted by those who spend a lot of time "outside the wire," meaning outside the protection of bases during combat missions. While on combat operations, food typically comes in the form of "MREs" or Meals, Ready-to-Eat. And while this food is "ready to eat," few find them appetizing, especially after days of eating them. These two Marines, having just returned from combat in Afghanistan's Helmand Province, enjoy some much-deserved hot, cook-prepared chow at sunset at Forward Operating Base Marjah.

To make the image, I used a Canon 80–200mm f/2.8 telephoto zoom lens on one of my Canon EOS-1Ds Mark III bodies, and composed a vertical shot at 150mm. I exposed for the highlights, so the Marines strongly contrasted against the shadowed background.

Racing Through the Storm

Hindu Kush of Eastern Afghanistan's Kunar Province

The Sikorsky UH-60 Black Hawk helicopter ranks among the most important, most trusted, and most used of the "work horses" of the modern U.S. military. Fast and nimble, the Black Hawk serves a number of roles, from air ambulance to troop transport. While Sikorsky has manufactured the UH-60 in a number of configurations, such as the Navy's Sea Hawk and the Air Force Special Operations Command's Pave Hawk, the U.S. Army's Black Hawk is the most ubiquitous. During Operation Enduring Freedom, Black Hawks flew throughout Afghanistan, supporting troops operating on low, flat desert terrain, to the highest battlefields in the country's mountainous east. Seen here, a Black Hawk races through a storm in the rugged Hindu Kush near the border with Pakistan during a storm. I captured this image from Forward Operating Base Monti, near the village of Asmar, in Afghanistan's Kunar Province.

I used one of my Canon EOS-1Ds Mark III bodies with an 80–200mm f/2.8 telephoto zoom lens set at 200mm to frame the Black Hawk amid the soaring peaks and ridges and churning clouds.

Forward Operating Base at Night

Helmand Province of Afghanistan

Sometimes being in a war zone can prove just plain quiet and uneventful—despite the ever present danger of an inbound rocket or mortar barrage. One restless and sleepless night at a forward operating base in Afghanistan's Helmand Province, while waiting for word to head out on a combat patrol, I popped outside my tent for some fresh air. Always on the hunt for images that are emblematic of the modern war experience, I stared at what I came to know as a ho-hum scene of the base's GBOSS, or ground based operational surveillance system, and surrounding facilities. Because it was night, however, I realized in a flash that the scene *(bottom)* could prove intriguing and dynamic. I set up one of my Canon EOS-1Ds Mark III bodies with a 24mm f/1.4 lens on a Gitzo carbon fiber tripod with a RRS ball head, and exposed for seventeen minutes.

The exposure captured the core of the base with a backdrop of star trails, as well as the lights of troops walking past the scene.

Tanker-in-Training

Marine Corps Air Ground Combat Center, Twentynine Palms, California

The M1A1 Abrams main battle tank ranks as one of the most imposing and intimidating implements of modern war. They're big, heavy, and loud. Despite being crewed by four highly-trained personnel, these "tankers," as they're called, rarely emerge from the heavily-armored beast they operate. Just after sunrise one morning, at the Marine Corps Air Ground Combat Center in California's Mojave Desert, I happened upon a great scene *(top):* a tanker-in-training, at the top of the Abrams, manning the .50 caliber machine gun. A rising sun partially silhouetted the scene, which I captured with a Nikon F6 film camera using a 70–200mm telephoto zoom lens on Fujichrome Velvia (ISO 100) film.

Refueling the Hornet

Above the Al Anbar Province of Iraq

During almost every military operation in the wars in Afghanistan and Iraq, air support ranked as one of the remarkably important components for troops on the ground. One of the most vital of the spectrum of air support missions flown was close air support, where at a moments notice, a helicopter or jet can swoop down and engage the enemy with bombs, rockets, missiles, or powerful guns. To stay overhead of the troops for hours at a time, jets like this Marine Corps F/A-18D Hornet, loaded with 20mm high explosive bullets and laser guided bombs, "tank" with aerial refueling aircraft multiple times during a mission.

I photographed this Hornet from the loading ramp of a KC-130J Super Hercules aircraft at dusk. I used a Nikon D200 camera with a 50mm f/1.4 lens.

FOB Dog

Forward Operating Base Monti, Eastern Afghanistan's Kunar Province

Outside of those trained specifically for combat operations, the U.S. military strictly forbids dogs on military bases in war zones—officially, that is. In small, far-flung forward operating bases or "FOBs" and the smaller combat outposts, however, commanders often turn a blind eye to troops, allowing local stray dogs to move into their confines. Life "on the inside" for these canines is typically much better than on the outside. They get good food (on a regular basis), and they get lots of attention. At FOB Monti, in eastern Afghanistan's Kunar Province, soldiers and Marines took care of a few of these dogs—and the dogs, in turn, took care of the troops in helping them to relax and get a few moments of "escape time." I photographed this Army SAW (squad automatic weapon) gunner smoking a cigarette and petting one of the base's "FOB dogs" after he returned from a difficult combat operation.

I captured the scene using one of my Canon EOS-1Ds Mark III bodies with a 300mm f/2.8 telephoto lens attached—the long telephoto lens allowed me to keep my distance and not intrude on the moment.

Super Stallion Maintenance

Camp Bastion, Helmand Province of Afghanistan

The largest helicopter that flew in the wars in Afghanistan and Iraq was the Sikorsky CH-53E Super Stallion helicopter. It's a three-engine, heavy lift helicopter that can haul tens of thousands of pounds of gear and dozens of troops for hundreds of miles. Not only is it massive, it's complex, requiring specialized maintenance by highly trained personnel. To get an up-close image of three of these maintainers working on the Super Stallion's main rotor hub, I used a 300mm f/2.8 lens on one of my Canon EOS-1Ds Mark III bodies and shot from a position that granted a clear view of each of them and the complex machine they kept safely operational.

Mountain Sniper Training

Marine Corps Mountain Warfare Training Center, near Bridgeport, California

In the wars in Afghanistan and Iraq, sniper teams played some of the most important—if little known—roles in combat operations. While snipers conduct a wide range of missions—many related to surveillance—they are most known for accurately shooting from well-concealed hides at long distances. Different environments require different skill sets and equipment for the highly specialized field of sniping. In mountainous Afghanistan, sniper operations proved some of the most difficult, especially in winter conditions. Here, sniper Joe Roy trains for such situations at the Marine Corps Mountain Warfare Training Center, high in the Sierra Nevada of eastern California.

I was able to get an up close shot of Joe, whom I first met in Afghanistan, and his M40A5 sniper rifle, by using one of my Canon EOS-1Ds Mark III bodies fitted with an 80–200mm telephoto zoom lens. I aimed straight at him, focusing on the muzzle of the gun, and he aimed straight at me. The rifle wasn't loaded.

Home is a long, long way off, both geographically and in spirit when deployed to places like the Al Anbar Province of Iraq. With constant threat of attack at all hours of the day and night, troops always welcomed any little "piece of home" with open arms. Mail delivery at the smaller bases was never regular, but when it came, it often came in volume. With the U.S. Postal Service offering inexpensive shipping, personnel received anything and everything that could fit into standard-sized boxes.

I got a wide angle view of Marines unloading a shipment using a Nikon F6 film camera with a 17–35mm f/2.8 lens on Fujichrome Velvia Film (ISO 100).

Mail Delivery

Haditha Region
of Iraq's Al Anbar Province

Manning the Chinook's Ramp Gun

East of Bagram Airfield, Afghanistan

The CH-47 Chinook ranks as one of the greatest military aircraft ever produced. The Chinook is fast, nimble, can carry a lot of troops and cargo, and it's well armed. A typical defensive configuration for a U.S. Army CH-47D Chinook, like the one pictured here, has two door machine guns—one on each side—and a machine gun mounted on the loading ramp of the helicopter. I shot this image of the aircraft's flight engineer manning the ramp gun as we sped over badland formations east of Bagram Airfield.

I photographed the moment using a Nikon F5 film camera with a 70–200mm f/2.8 telephoto zoom lens on Fujichrome Velvia (ISO 50) film. I exposed for the bright landscape below, casting the flight engineer and his weapon as a silhouette. My first flight on a helicopter of any type, military or civilian, I'll never forget that photo shoot as we sped over eastern Afghanistan.

USS Peleliu at Dusk

Pacific Ocean
off the Coast of northern
San Diego County, California

The U.S. military constantly trains for all types of war, even during times of ongoing conflict. The USS Peleliu, one of the U.S. Navy's amphibious assault ships, deployed throughout the world during the wars in Afghanistan and Iraq, supporting combat operations as well as training. Seen here at dusk, the Peleliu supports a Marine Corps training operation at Camp Pendleton, California, in northern San Diego County. The Navy decommissioned the Peleliu in 2015.

I shot this image with a Nikon F6 film camera fitted with a 200–400 f/4 lens on Fujichrome Velvia film (ISO 100).

Passers-By

Helmand Province
of Afghanistan

Much of the war in Afghanistan was fought as a counterinsurgency, a band of the spectrum of warfare where troops sought to root out insurgents and terrorists and simultaneously build trust with non-combatant locals. It often proves incredibly difficult and frustrating, as insurgents can blend in with the local population. When I was embedded on combat operations and we passed by locals (or they passed by us), especially children, I always wondered what was going through their minds. While partially concealed in a ditch in the Helmand Province of Afghanistan, I heard some children approach. They noticed us, but they didn't seem to really care. I quickly composed a telephoto view of the three of them as they passed through shadows of tree branches under which we had taken cover a few minutes earlier.

With an 80–200mm f/2.8 telephoto zoom lens mounted to one of my Canon EOS-1Ds Mark III bodies, I waited till the shadows framed their eyes, and shot a burst of ten exposures, this one turning out the best. I'll always wonder what they were thinking as they passed us by.

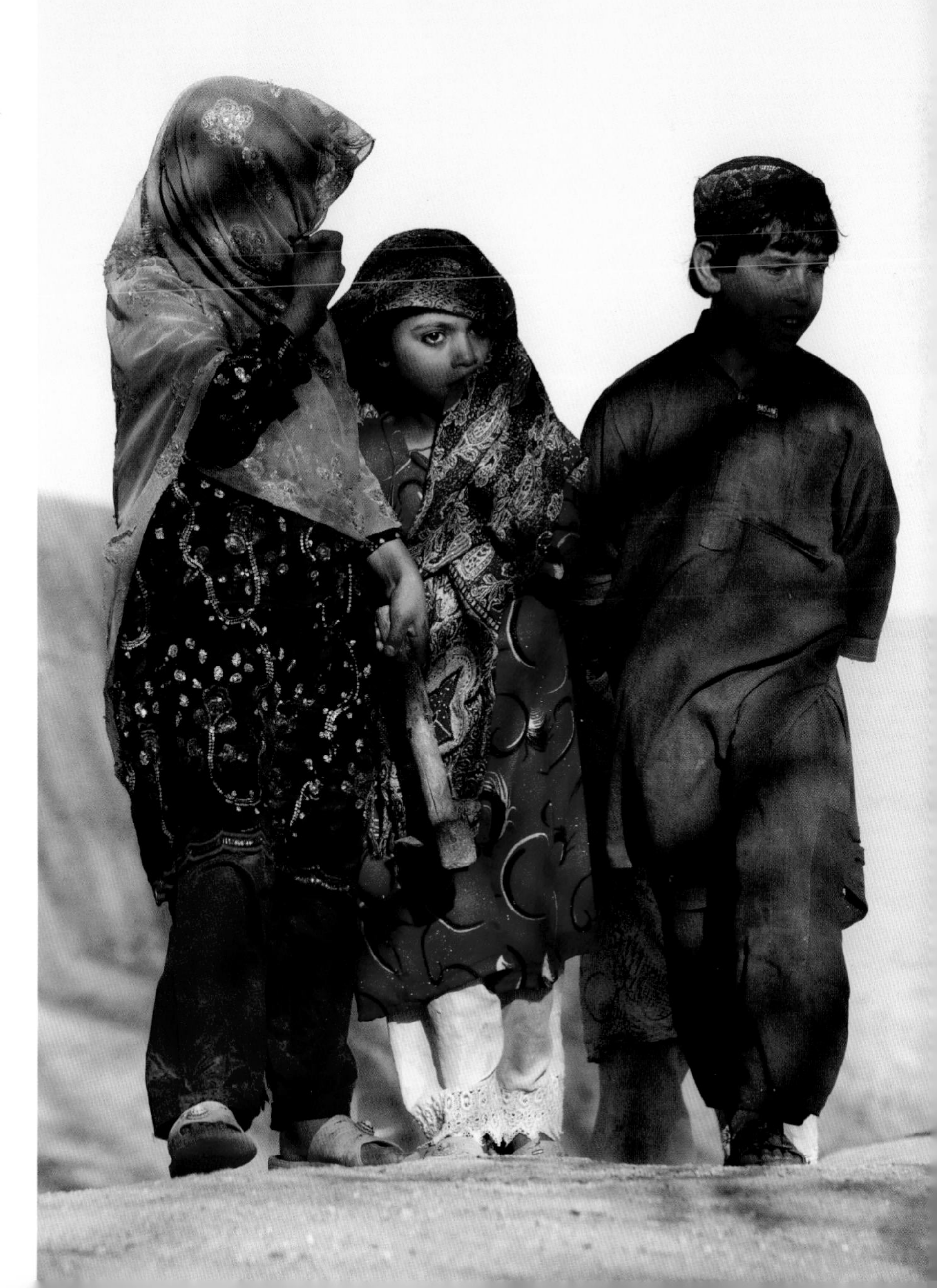

Harrier Pilot Prepares for Launch

Al Asad Airbase, Al Anbar Province of Iraq

Prior to embarking on all of my combat embeds, I would always ponder the different types of images that I'd like to capture, a process many photographers call "pre-visualization." But war is incredibly dynamic, and scenes, lighting, and of course, safety levels, can change in a fraction of a second. Ever aware of this, I was always on the lookout for images of opportunity, moments that I hadn't pondered before, but which would emerge before my eyes. This was one such moment, a Marine Corps AV-8B Harrier II pilot preparing to launch in the morning hours from Al Asad Airbase in Iraq's Al Anbar Province. I was on the ramp as the pilot and ground crew prepared the aircraft for launch, and as I jogged around the screaming jet, my eyes locked onto this scene of concentration and purpose.

My 70–200mm f/2.8 lens, attached to a Nikon D200, followed my eyes, and I was able to create this unexpected image.

Geared Up

Forward Operating Base Wright, Asadabad, Kunar Province of eastern Afghanistan

I spent most of my time in the Pech River Valley region of Afghanistan's eastern Kunar Province during my first combat embed. The region was extremely active with enemy activity, including improvised explosive device (IED) attacks. Just prior to "pushing out" on a large convoy that would take us along a stretch of dirt road known as "IED Alley," I grabbed a favorite camera of mine, a Pentax 67 II. The 67 is a big, bulky, heavy medium-format film camera, but I loved it and brought it with me to Afghanistan. I rarely used it during combat operations due to its weight and bulk, but loved it for candid portraits, among other types of images. With a 105mm lens attached, I eyed this Marine all "geared up" and ready to head into the great unknown of the start of a combat operation. I shot it on Fujichrome Velvia film (ISO 50).

Desert Launch

Marine Corps Air Ground Combat Center, Twentynine Palms, California

"We train like we fight" is a statement I've heard from members of all branches of the U.S. military. The aphorism, rooted in necessity for maximum readiness, governs all aspects of training, including environmental acclimatization. The Marine Corps Air Ground Combat Center, located deep in the Mojave Desert of California, proved vital for troops deploying to the arid environment of Iraq as well as the desert regions of Afghanistan during the wars there. Desert environments pose a spectrum of threats, some of the greatest being "brown outs," where helicopter rotor wash kicks up a storm of dust at unimproved landing zones. Here, a Marine Corps CH-46E Sea Knight, known by the Marines as the "Phrog," lands in a cloud of kicked-up dust at the Training Center.

I photographed the Phrog with a Nikon F6 film camera using a 70–200mm f/2.8 lens on Fujichrome Velvia film (ISO 100).

Door Kick

Haditha,
Al Anbar Province
of Iraq

Despite continuous advances in the military's ability to gather and process intelligence, and hence an ever expanding capability to know as much about a battlespace as possible, the unknown still remains an ever-present component of war. During a combat patrol in the dangerous city of Haditha, Iraq, the squad with which I was embedded got word of a possible Al Qaeda weapons cache in an abandoned safe house. Was the intel correct? Was the squad being led to an ambush or a booby trap? A quick reconnoiter around the house's perimeter proved inconclusive and the front door was locked. There was only one way to proceed—kick it open.

Bracing myself for a possible explosion, or ambush from within, I held my Nikon F6 film camera with a 17–35mm f/2.8 lens against my ballistic goggles, and fired a continuous burst of exposures on Fujichrome Velvia (ISO 100) as the Marine kicked open the front door. I then joined other members of the squad in a rush inside. The home was completely empty.

Apache in Flight

Jalalabad, Nangarhar Province, Afghanistan

All four branches of the U.S. military possess aircraft capable of supporting ground troops. The Army's AH-64 Apache ranks among the most potent. Bristling with an array of weapons, and a powerful scanner to pick out targets from miles away, the Apache is one of the most welcome sights to ground troops.

I photographed this one at Jalalabad, Afghanistan, as it approached a landing zone. I used a Nikon F5 film camera with a 70–200mm f/2.8 telephoto zoom lens and Fujichrome Velvia (ISO 50) film. I used a shutter priority setting to meter the scene, and selected 1/125 second—fast enough to keep all of the helicopter but the rotor blades sharp, but slow enough to allow those rotor blades to show "sweep" on the image.

Afghan Fighter at Dawn

Hindu Kush of the Kunar Province of Afghanistan

Many combat operations in both Iraq and Afghanistan included local forces. This served a dual purpose: for U.S. forces to train them, and for these local forces to aid Americans, primarily with local knowledge and intelligence gathering. During one such operation in eastern Afghanistan's Kunar Province, a select group of indigenous fighters called the Afghan Security Forces, or ASF, fought alongside U.S. Marines in the Hindu Kush just outside the village of Nangalam.

As we moved higher on an unnamed mountain to close on a remote village suspected of harboring Al Qaeda fighters, one of the ASF jumped up on a rock outcrop. As he shouldered his AK-47 and scanned the distance, I quickly composed an image of him and the surrounding landscape with a Nikon F6 film camera using a 17–35mm f/2.8 lens. I exposed a number of images of the scene on Fujichrome Velvia (ISO 50) film, being careful to position myself to ensure that he was well contrasted against the glowing sky.

Behind Bulletproof Glass

Al Anbar Province of Iraq

"Standing post," a military colloquialism for guard duty, can—and often does—prove to be one of the most monotonous tasks in the military. It can also be one of the most dangerous. Throughout the war in Iraq, highly trained enemy snipers unexpectedly struck personnel standing post. The solution was the emplacement of bulletproof glass on watch towers. In one incident, however, a sniper fired through a two-inch space where pieces of the glass leaned against each other, killing the guard as he walked past the narrow slit.

I photographed this scene just as the sun broke the horizon, as the guard scanned a city scene before him. I used a Nikon F6 film camera with a 17–35mm f/2.8 lens and Fujichrome Velvia (ISO 100) film.

Yodaville at Night

Urban Target Complex
(R-2301-West)
Yuma, Arizona

On maps it's "Urban Target Complex (R-2301-West)." To those who train at this location south of Yuma, Arizona, in the scorching desert, it's "Yodaville." Named after the call sign of Major Floyd Usry, "Yoda," a Marine Corps AH-1W SuperCobra gunship pilot who first envisioned the Urban Target Complex, this "town" in the desert has never been inhabited, nor will it ever be. It's designed to be bombed and shot at with rockets, missiles, and bullets from low flying helicopter gunships and ground attack jets for urban close air support training. Yodaville is built of steel shipping containers, stacked in some places four-high, and it's laid out in a fashion similar to towns and villages in Iraq and Afghanistan. I spent a few days and nights at Yodaville during live fire training—positioned sometimes as close as 300 meters.

Live fire training is exciting, and it's loud, and it makes for great photographs day and night. I captured this night-time image of tracer rounds and rockets slamming into Yodaville with star trails in the background using a tripod-mountain Nikon D300 with a 17–35mm f/2.8 lens for a five minute exposure.

A View From Above

Over the Al Anbar Province of Iraq

Aircraft of all types bring a tremendous array of capabilities to a combat operation, from close air support with rockets, guns, missiles, and bombs, to medical evacuation. One of the most notable of these capabilities is simple perspective: aircraft provide a view from above—a bird's eye view—and that high view, even a few dozen feet above the ground, brings so much more into plain sight than do eyes that are chained by gravity to the ground. Concealed enemy fighters, obscured supply lines, and recently disturbed dirt—indicating a possible hidden cache of weapons or an improvised explosive device—jump into view from the air. During a flight in a UH-1N Iroquois helicopter over the Al Anbar Province of Iraq during a close air support mission, I watched as the aircraft's crew chief, manning a .50 caliber machine gun, carefully scanned the desert landscape below. With a 12–24mm zoom lens mounted to a Nikon D200, I focused on the crew chief but exposed for the landscape below, partially silhouetting him as he scanned for enemy activity.

Muzzle Nest

East of Kabul, Afghanistan

War zones, both past and present—and in this case, a war zone that was both present and past—are filled with surprises. While temporarily at a base used by both conventional and special operations personnel, I took some time to roam around a "bone yard" of old equipment discarded from the Soviet-Afghan war located adjacent the facility. I found old tanks, dilapidated Scud missiles, transport trucks, and lines of old, rusted artillery pieces. As I walked by one of the howitzers, a little bird caught my eye—flying into the muzzle of the gun. A careful look revealed that the bird had made a nest in the howitzer's muzzle! Moving slowly so as not to disturb it, I attached my 300mm f/2.8 lens to one of my EOS-1Ds Mark III bodies, then composed a series of vertical shots. The bird let me photograph it for just a few seconds before launching back into the air. It shouldn't have been much of a surprise, as life of all forms goes on, even in war zones, and in this case, assisted by discarded implements of combat.

There is no such thing in the military as "toughness training," not formally, that is. But if there was, it would be timed for a blizzard at the Marine Corps Mountain Warfare Training Center, or MWTC, located in the high Sierra Nevada mountains of eastern California. Members of all services go to the MWTC to learn and hone mountain and winter combat and survival skills. Some of the courses they run at the base last for weeks, and when storms strike, there's no retreating. Many of the students of the MWTC leaned on skills they acquired at the base while deployed to the mountains of Afghanistan. One of the most important attributes engendered at the MWTC, however, comes through the forced acclimatization to raw austerity—no matter how tough a situation, summoning the will to survive in a blizzard during combat training imbues the ability to adapt to the cruelest of environments, of any type. I shot this photograph with a Canon EOS-1Ds Mark III body fitted with an 80–200mm f/2.8 telephoto zoom lens.

Toughness Training

Marine Corps Mountain Warfare Training Center, near Bridgeport, California

Up Close with the Osprey

Over the Kandahar Province of Afghanistan

After decades in development, the V-22 Osprey debuted not only as a new aircraft, but a new type of aircraft, a tiltrotor. An operational fusion of a helicopter and a fixed-wing aircraft, the Osprey launches and lands vertically like a helicopter, and races along in horizontal flight like a propeller-driven airplane. In early 2010 I embedded with VMM-261, or Marine Medium Tiltrotor Squadron 261, during the first combat deployment of the MV-22 to Afghanistan. During some of the many flights I took on the Osprey during my two weeks with the squadron, I was fortunate to be able to coordinate some air-to-air shoots. Flying out of Kandahar Province one afternoon, I sat on the loading ramp with a crew chief as a second Osprey pulled in tight for a few seconds, granting an incredible perspective of a new "bird of war" in action. I photographed this Osprey with one of my Canon EOS-1Ds Mark III bodies fitted with an 80–200mm f/2.8 lens at 200mm. I set the camera for shutter priority and set the shutter speed for 1/200 of a second, which would keep the body of the Osprey sharp, but allow for just enough "sweep" of the proprotors at 200mm to show their rotation.

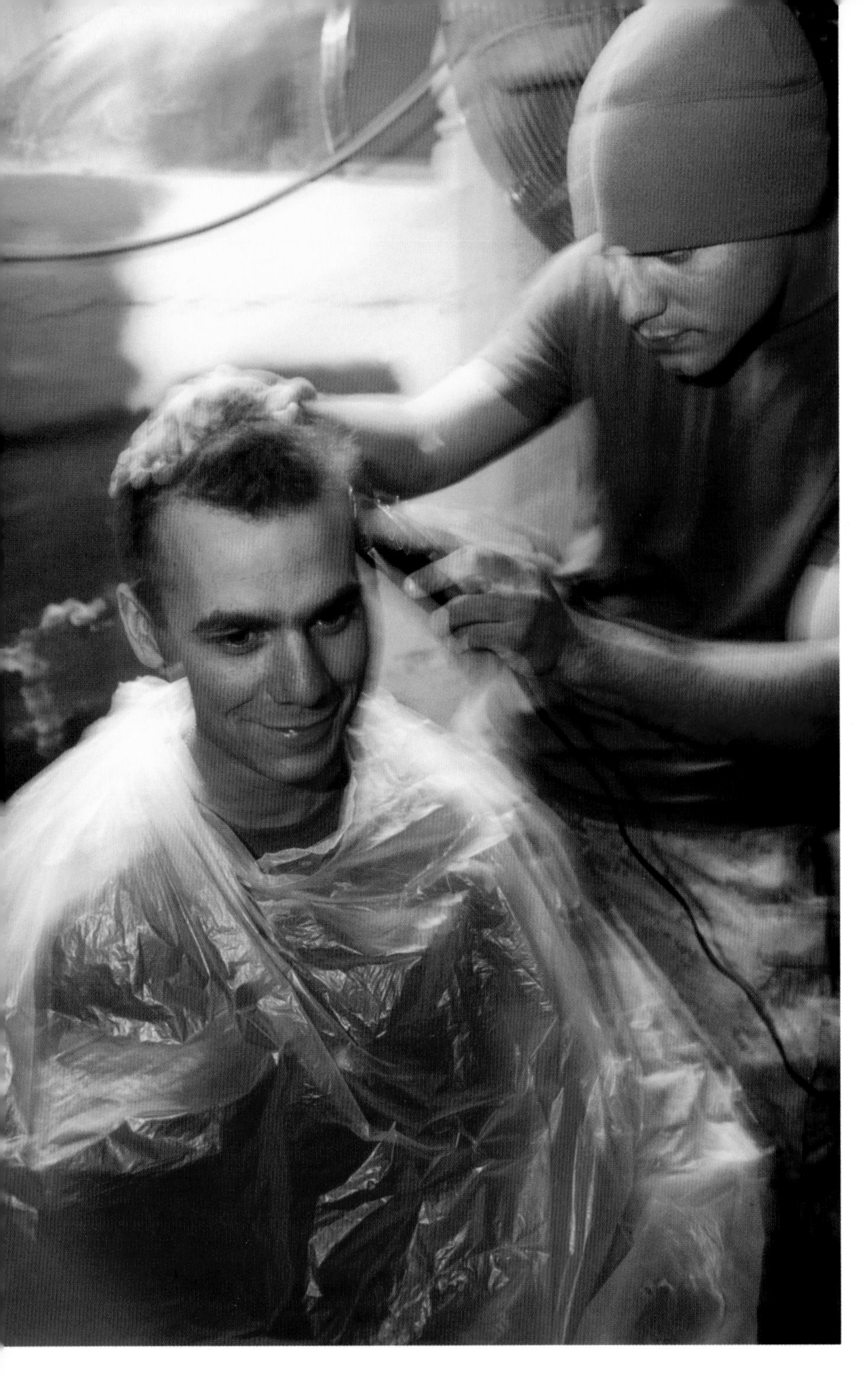

True "down time" doesn't exist in combat, not even during sleep. Furthermore, the military requires everyone to adhere to strict standards, including hair length and other attributes related to appearance and grooming. Among the time required to carry out their primary jobs, eat, and sleep, members of the military need to find time—or make time—to keep "within regs."

In this image, a Marine gives another Marine a haircut late at night at a remote, frequently-attacked combat outpost in the Al Anbar Province of Iraq. I shot this with a Nikon F6 film camera using a 17–35mm zoom lens and Fujichrome Velvia (ISO 100) film. I shot it with a Nikon Speedlight using rear-curtain flash sync.

Hair to Standards

Al Anbar Province of Iraq

Mounted Patrol

Border of Kunar and Nuristan Provinces, eastern Afghanistan

Steep, rugged terrain and poor roads added tremendously to the challenges of waging war in Afghanistan, particularly in the eastern part of the country. I was embedded with a platoon of Marines when they received time-critical intelligence about a weapons cache located deep inside one of the most remote aspects of Afghanistan about ten miles distant. We left the base soon thereafter on a "mounted patrol," meaning we moved by vehicles—a convoy of Humvees. The route deteriorated quickly on our journey to a tiny enclave outside the village of Wanat, which lies in the Waygal Valley on the border of the eastern Afghan provinces of Kunar and Nuristan. Cut into the side of a mountain, with threats of improvised explosive devices along every inch of the dirt road, the dusty, narrow, and rutted route started out bad, and only got worse.

I shot this image with a Nikon F6 film camera and a 17–35mm f/2.8 lens on Fujichrome Velvia (ISO 50) film just before we could go no farther. Then we walked.

Scanning the Distance

Helmand Province of Afghanistan

I pondered this shot for what seemed like hours. I was embedded with Marines during a combat operation outside a small village in the Helmand Province of Afghanistan. There was a lot of enemy activity in the region, and exposing myself for more than a few seconds to take a photograph could have ended in a bad way. So while it seemed like hours, it was probably less than a couple minutes. Intense concentration on the myriad dynamic factors requisite to create a bold, striking photograph that I realized could emerge before my eyes combined with piercing awareness of the danger of the moment was exhilarating, but also exhausting. I really just wanted to crouch against a mud wall, toss my body armor and helmet on the dirt, and take a nap. But I didn't. As the sun rose, and the air warmed—and I started really sweating from the heat and the moment—I could see how all visual components were converging for the image I craved. I sprang up and hopped into just the right point in the geometry of the scene with my Canon EOS-1Ds Mark III with an 80–200mm f/2.8 lens attached, and nailed this image of a Marine scanning for any enemy activity—the sunburst emblematic of his acuity of purpose. Then I slouched against the safety of a mud wall with the wholehearted intent of taking a nap. But I didn't. The Marines kept moving, and so did I.

Abrams at Rest

Al Anbar Province of Iraq

I shot this image of two M1A1 Abrams main battle tanks just before dusk at the end of a large combat operation in a remote part of Iraq's Al Anbar Province. Loading into a large troop transport truck, I turned to see these two tanks at the top of a distant rise with the waters of Lake Qadisiyah in the background. Despite the power and destructive capability of the two M1A1s, the scene struck me as tranquil and relaxing. I'll never know, but I wondered if the tank crews had been sleeping.

I carefully framed the Abrams with a Nikon F6 film camera attached to a tripod-mounted 200–400mm lens set at 400mm and focused on the foreground tank. I shot the image on Fujichrome Velvia (ISO 100) film.

Leaping from the Herc

Alpena Combat Readiness Training Center, Michigan

Train, train, and then train some more—it's a foundational axiom of readiness the American military embraces. Units repeatedly undertake the most dangerous exercises like live fire training and leaping from low-flying aircraft to always be prepared. Here, a special operations team leaps from a C-130 Hercules to practice their role in the seizure of an airfield. It's one thing to jump out of an airplane, it's something very much more serious and difficult to jump out at low level with nearly 100 pounds of gear attached. A lot can go wrong with all those parachutes in the air, and then a lot can go wrong upon meeting the ground laden with all that gear.

I shot this image using a Nikon F6 film camera with a 200–400mm f/4 lens and Fujichrome Velvia (ISO 100) film.

Flag Before the Storm

Helmand Province, of Afghanistan

Some of the most dangerous weather conditions that U.S. troops faced in both Afghanistan and Iraq didn't involve rain, snow, ice, or even fog, but sand and dust. Sand storms and dust storms (sometimes called haboobs) could severely hamper both ground and air operations, choking visibility to just a few feet, and causing maintenance issues with all sorts of equipment from rifles to jet engines (and my cameras). Hot, dry winds saturated with blinding, gritty, choking dust often forced troops to stop in place and wait till the storm passed—and many lasted for days. Near the end of an operation in which I was embedded in Afghanistan's Helmand Province, we saw a dust storm approaching—so we hurried up and finished the mission by sprinting back toward base, just a few miles distant. We arrived just before the dust did, allowing me to take this photograph of the wind blowing an American flag as the approaching dust just began to choke out the sun. I photographed the scene with one of my Canon EOS-1Ds Mark III bodies with an 80–200mm telephoto zoom lens.

Nothing to See in the Movie Theater

Haditha, Al Anbar Province of Iraq

During a combat operation that took Marines through an abandoned and dilapidated oil refinery town, I accompanied a squad leader into an old movie theater. Much of the other buildings had been pocked with bullets, mortars, and artillery fire, but the theater was mostly intact, assailed only by time itself. "Nothing here to see," the squad leader said to me after a minute, referring to enemy activity or possible weapons caches. We then looked at each other and broke out laughing at the irony of him making that statement in a theater.

I photographed him with a Nikon F6 film camera with a 17–35mm lens on Fujichrome Velvia (ISO 100) film, and we moved on.

Afghan Fighter on Rock Pinnacle

Kunar Province of Afghanistan

The Afghan Security Forces, or ASF, consisted of Afghan fighters aligned with American and coalition forces in the war

in Afghanistan. The ASF, like the Afghan National Army and the Afghan National Police, worked and fought side-by-side with U.S. forces, and in many cases received training, weapons, and even uniforms from the Americans. The ASF proved tremendously helpful in the war effort, particularly in the mountainous, remote eastern reaches of the country, as they either had ongoing relationships with locals, or could easily forge friendships. Seen here is one of the ASF fighters, wearing a Marine Corps issued uniform, holding his AK-47, and wearing shoes that the Marines would definitely not consider suitable for rock climbing. But during one combat operation, that's just what he did in order to get a better look over some nearby boulders that we needed to round.

I photographed him with a Nikon F6 film camera with a 70–200mm zoom lens on Fujichrome Velvia (ISO 50) film.

Hornets in Formation

South China Sea, near Kuantan, Malaysia

In 2009 my friend Doug Pasnik offered me an incredible opportunity: document his Marine Corps F/A-18D Hornet Squadron during an air-to-air combat training exercise with the Royal Malaysian Air Force. I queried Smithsonian's *Air & Space* magazine, and they immediately expressed interest in sending me along. It proved an incredible example of how while wars continued to rage in Afghanistan and Iraq, the U.S. military constantly trains for all types of potential future conflicts, even ones very different in nature than current conflicts. During my month with the squadron, VMFA(AW)-121 (Marine Fighter Attack Squadron (All Weather)-121), I completed five air-to-air shoots of Marine Corps Hornets and Malaysian MiG-29 Fulcrums, all from the open ramp of a

Marine Corps KC-130J Super Hercules refueling aircraft. Many of the American pilots had recently flown in combat in Iraq and Afghanistan, and many would deploy to those theaters subsequent to this training—but as I learned, all training is relevant, even though it may not be used in current wars (Al Qaeda and the Taliban didn't have fighter jets, but the Russians, Chinese, and North Koreans do).

Hornet Versus MiG

South China Sea, near Kuantan, Malaysia

During my month with the squadron, VMFA(AW)-121, Marine Fighter Attack Squadron (All Weather)-121, I completed five air-to-air shoots of Marine Corps Hornets and Malaysian MiG-29 Fulcrums (facing page and above), all from the open ramp of a Marine Corps KC-130J Super Hercules refueling aircraft. Photographing the Hornets in formation with the MiGs was both exhilarating and somewhat historic. The two types of aircraft, each designed by arch foes in the throes of the Cold War, were intended to knock each other out of the sky, not cooperatively fly together through the heights.

Into the Pech

Kunar Province of Afghanistan

The Pech River Valley of eastern Afghanistan is a region of incredible beauty and history—notably, history of war. The Pech and surrounding mountains and valleys, tucked into the heart of the storied Hindu Kush, saw some of the earliest and most infamous battles of the Soviet-Afghan War. The region also was the stage for some of the most notable missions of Operation Enduring Freedom, including Operation Red Wings, which tragically saw the demise of 19 U.S. special operations personnel on June 28, 2005.

Early one morning at the end of a combat operation that took place just a few months after Red Wings at a location just a few miles from where the tragedy occurred, I positioned myself to capture both the beauty of the valley and military history continuing to be made. Still in the shadows as the sun rose, I photographed this Marine as he descended toward the floor of the Pech using a Nikon F6 film camera with a 17–35mm f/2.8 zoom lens and Fujichrome Velvia (ISO 50) film.

Willie Pete

Kunar Province of Afghanistan

In 2005 when I arrived at Firebase Blessing (also called Camp Blessing), located deep in the Pech River Valley of Afghanistan's Kunar Province, the Marines stationed there gave me a crash course in combat. One of the lessons was that the Taliban and Al Qaeda used white phosphorous mortar rounds in their attacks in the region. White Phosphorous (nicknamed "Willie Pete") munitions rank as some of the most insidious and cruel weapons ever developed. Upon impact, a shell or mortar containing Willie Pete explodes, sending chunks of the material in all directions. As soon as these chunks come in contact with air, they burn a blinding yellow color and emit pungent, dense white smoke. Anything Willie Pete hits burns until the chemical reaction ceases—when no more white phosphorous remains. It can't be extinguished by any normal means, and it burns through just about everything, including skin, bone, and even armor. The Marines of Firebase Blessing captured a lot of Willie Pete during their raids, and then promptly disposed of it with controlled detonations, or "controlled dets."

I photographed this det with a Nikon F6 film camera using a 70–200mm f/2.8 telephoto zoom lens at 200mm, allowing me to stay far away from the explosion. Good riddance.

Combat Engineers

Helmand Province of Afghanistan

Combat engineers, a little known MOS, or military occupational specialty, perform many important tasks, including building bridges, walls, berms, temporary buildings, and a host of other construction applications. They're also tasked with finding hidden enemy explosives and other weapons, and then very dramatically disposing of them in controlled detonations. In addition to a standard combat load, combat engineers often carry metal detectors and small shovels to aid in their searches for enemy wares. Often working at the very front lines of combat, they carry out some of the most dangerous missions in the military, day in, and day out.

I photographed these two combat engineers at the end of a large operation in Afghanistan's Helmand Province. A dust storm was approaching, and I just didn't have enough natural light to get a good candid portrait without blur, so I used rear curtain flash sync with my Canon EOS-1Ds Mark III and 16–35mm f/2.8 zoom lens. The effect worked—the combination of muted light of the early evening, the dust in the sky, and just enough blur and fill flash made for a great capture of a memorable ⅓ of a second.

F-15E Strike Eagle

Bagram Airfield, Afghanistan

When McDonnell Douglas (now Boeing) first developed the renowned F-15 Eagle, designers focused entirely on an aircraft for the air superiority/supremacy mission set, meaning air-to-air or "dogfighting," to defeat an enemy air force, in the air. They paid little to no attention to the ground attack capabilities combat aircraft can undertake. The U.S. Military, as well as McDonnell Douglas, quickly realized that the airframe could perform a second role—ground attack, and the F-15E Strike Eagle was born. The aircraft made major contributions at the very beginning of both the war in Afghanistan and the war in Iraq, and throughout both conflicts continued to prove its importance to overall campaigns.

I photographed this Strike Eagle with one of my Canon EOS-1Ds Mark III bodies with an 80–200mm f/2.8 telephoto zoom lens, mounted atop a Gitzo carbon fiber tripod and a RRS ball head for 1.3 seconds. Artificial lighting in the foreground balanced perfectly with the background light of dusk. The pilot emerged from the cockpit after a mission at just the right time for me to capture him walking away from the aircraft.

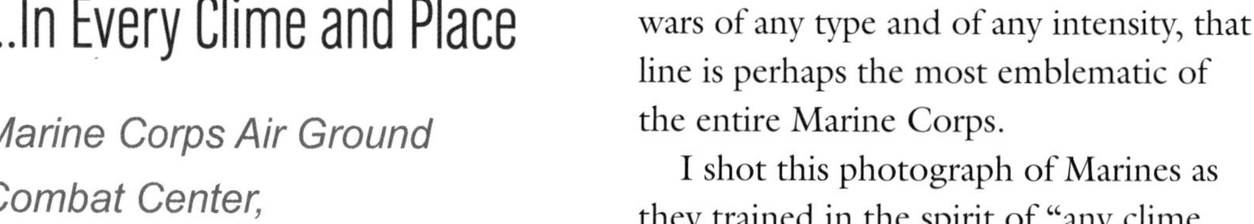

...In Every Clime and Place

Marine Corps Air Ground Combat Center, Twentynine Palms, California

The oldest official song in the U.S. Armed forces is the Marines' Hymn. It's a famous song that begins with "From the Halls of Montezuma...." One of the most salient lines of the Hymn is the third line of the second verse, which reads "We have fought in every clime and place." Able to be deployed anywhere in the world at a moment's notice to fight wars of any type and of any intensity, that line is perhaps the most emblematic of the entire Marine Corps.

I shot this photograph of Marines as they trained in the spirit of "any clime and place." I was atop OP (observation point) Left, at the Marine Corps Air Ground Combat Center, at Twentynine Palms, California, and eyed this AAV-P7/A1 amphibious assault vehicle, or "amtrack," approaching. The amtrack can launch from a ship at sea, hit the beach, and then keep on going—into any clime or place, with Marine fighter and attack jets overhead, and Marine artillery right behind them, flanked by Marine Abrams tanks.

I shot this image with a Nikon F6 film camera and a 200–400mm f/4 zoom lens with Fujichrome Velvia (ISO 100) film.

The Apache's Most Important Components

Jalalabad, Nangarhar Province, Afghanistan

I've shot more than a thousand photographs of Army AH-64 Apache gunships in war zones, and this one ranks as my favorite. Why? Because it clearly shows the most important elements of the Apache, the pilots. With myriad weapons, communications, and sensor

platforms—in addition to basic flight controls—the Apache is one of the most difficult aircraft, of any type, to operate. The level of skill and dedication required to fly Apaches is tremendous. Flying Apaches also carries a substantial level of risk. They are not "flying tanks" as some have called them (there is no such thing, as tank-like armor simply weighs too much to be put on an aircraft), but they do bristle with weapons desired by friendly ground forces for the Apaches to employ, like 30mm high explosive rounds, Hellfire missiles, and high explosive rockets. In addition to all of their flight and technical training, the most important trait of Apache pilots is their devotion to the ground war fighters they support. Apache lore teems with stories in both Afghanistan and Iraq of Apache pilots going to extremes to aid friendly forces on the ground.

I shot this image of an Apache during a refueling stop in Jalalabad, Afghanistan, with a Nikon F5 film camera and a 70–200mm f/2.8 lens with Fujichrome Velvia (ISO 50) film.

On the Hunt

Kunar Province of Eastern Afghanistan

With reliable word received of a nearby hidden enemy weapons cache, Marines with whom I was embedded at a small forward operating base in Afghanistan's Kunar Province jumped into action to check it out. One of these Marines, SAW (squad automatic weapon) gunner Mario Anes, who had just lit a cigarette, immediately hopped into a Humvee before anyone else in his squad. A minute later, the convoy roared outside the wire and we were headed for the unknown, or at best, the partially known.

As the convoy began, I got this shot of Mario, staring intensely ahead of us as we roared along. I used a Nikon F6 film camera with a 17–35mm f/2.8 zoom lens and Fujichrome Velvia (ISO 50) film.

Squad Circle

Haditha, Al Anbar Province of Iraq

The minutes leading up to leaving the relative safety of a base for a patrol or large operation always bring what seems like an exponentially elevated level of focus and seriousness. Weapons are checked, helmets and body armor are secured, and no jokes are told (well, sometimes they're told). Then comes the moment, and the wire is to your back. Just before leaving with this squad for a patrol of the city of Haditha, in the Al Anbar Province of Iraq, the squad had formed a tight circle to go over final points for the coming dangerous hours.

I got down on the ground, and with a Nikon F6 film camera with a 17–35mm f/2.8 zoom lens attached, made this image on Fujichrome Velvia (ISO 100) film.

Ascent Amid The Storm

Kunar Province of Eastern Afghanistan

While embedded in the Kunar Province of Afghanistan, near the border with Pakistan, I always kept an eye on the weather—out of vigilance as well as for artistic reasons. During certain months of the year, the Indian Monsoon (AKA South Asian Monsoon) brings moisture to the region, moisture that creates powerful, and oftentimes dangerous—but beautiful—thunderstorms. As I watched one build one late afternoon, and as the setting sun cast the roiling clouds in warm pink and golden tones, I noticed a small group of Afghan Security Forces members, who were co-located with American forces at a tiny base in the area, begin to ascend a mountainside to an observation post. With the fighters cast as silhouettes by the bright clouds, I framed the scene using a Nikon F6 film camera with a 200–400mm f/4 telephoto zoom lens and made a number of exposures on Fujichrome (ISO 50) film.

A Legend of Legends

Marine Corps Mountain Warfare Training Center, near Bridgeport, California

Of all the legendary war machines created throughout history, few have attained the level of profound influence and importance as the CH-47 Chinook helicopter. It can carry dozens of troops and tens of thousands of pounds of cargo, both internally and slung underneath it. It's fast—operationally the fastest helicopter in the U.S. military. It's powerful, able to hover at high altitudes even when heavily loaded. And it's nimble, with its tandem rotor configuration allowing pilots to put it precisely where they want it. My first flight ever in a helicopter was in a Chinook, in Afghanistan, and I'll never forget it. The Chinook quickly became one of my favorite military subjects to photograph, and this is one of my all time best images of the helicopter, showing it in its element—speeding through the cold air, high in the mountains. I photographed this CH-47, a D model, with a Nikon F5 film camera and a 70–200mm f/2.8 telephoto zoom lens using Fujichrome Velvia (ISO 50) film.

IED Sweep

Al Anbar Province of Iraq

Some of the most frightening moments for me in all my time embedded came in Iraq during "sweeps" for improvised explosive devices, or IEDs. Just the existence of a single IED in an area means that each excursion outside the relative safety of a base is one long close call, if nothing happens. And if one does go off, either by a tripping mechanism or by a hidden "trigger man" watching, lives can end, or at best, be changed for the worse forever. Keen eyes constantly looked out for any tiny clue for a hidden IED, and once spotted, convoys would come to a halt and then everyone, including me, would jump out and start taking closer looks. Sticking the camera to my face and hitting the shutter release relieved some of my tension. And every now and then a good picture came out—like this one that I shot at the end of a sweep. I took it with a Nikon F6 film camera and a 70–200mm f/2.8 telephoto zoom lens and Fujichrome Velvia (ISO 100) film.

Say RPG!

Hindu Kush of Kunar Province of Afghanistan

It's impossible to conjure all the events and sights that could possibly be experienced in war. And just like there are unimaginably frightening and horrible ones, there are also some unthinkably bizarre, and... hilarious ones, like this image *(right)*. The subject of the image is a member of the Afghan Security Forces, or ASF, who lived with a platoon of Marines at a small base in the Hindu Kush of Afghanistan's Kunar Province. He was an RPG (rocket propelled grenade) gunner, and apparently also a photographer. After a lightning insert of Marines and ASF onto the top of a grassy mountain, as the engines of the Chinook helicopters spun up into screams as the pilots prepared to lift off, this ASF member, holding a live, loaded rocket propelled grenade in one hand, pulled out a disposable film camera, and started snapping away. I photographed the photographer with a Nikon F6 film camera and a 17–35mm f/2.8 zoom lens using Fujichrome Velvia (ISO 50) film.

Insert

Kunar Province of Afghanistan

Over the years I've heard the phrase "your first deployment is your best deployment" many times. While I wasn't "deployed," but embedded, I definitely understand the sentiment and meaning behind that phrase, although I'd replace "best" with "vividly memorable." It stems, I think, from pondering the unknown of war, then facing it head on, and then making that unfamiliar the known by living it. That's what this photograph is all about for me. This was my first combat operation, and I was really excited, and really scared as those Chinooks brought us onto that mountain top. So I ran around and took pictures—and that helped me be not so terrified. But seeing the photographs years later brings it all back, ironically. In the foreground is Mike Scholl, Marine Corps machine gunner, and just to his rear is Luis Anaya, a member of an incredible cadre of war fighters, Navy Hospital Corpsmen—essentially medics, or "docs," some of whom, like Doc Anaya, attach to Marine Corps units that go to far away places like this one, teeming with Taliban and Al Qaeda.

I photographed this scene with a Nikon F6 film camera using a 17–35mm zoom lens and Fujichrome Velvia (ISO 50) film, and shot the image at 1/125 of a second to get the rotor sweeps of the Chinooks that just inserted us.

The War Fighter

Helmand Province of Afghanistan

When deployed into a combat theater, war fighters know that they need to be ready at a moment's notice for any eventuality, even when sleeping—incoming mortar fire, a patrol, a medical evacuation, anything. Simply put, war vastly eclipses all of humanity's other endeavors in terms of danger because other humans are actively working to kill and injure you and your compatriots. As such, as a human embedded with U.S. forces, I was always on the lookout for such dangers to me and to those around me, and as a photographer, I was always on the hunt for images that captured the spirit of vigilance, strength, purpose, and readiness that I saw in my surroundings. At the end of a combat operation in Afghanistan's Helmand Province, safely inside the perimeter of a forward operating base, I noticed a Marine scanning the distance through his gun sight. He'd seen something—I don't know what, and I didn't ask. The setting sun perfectly silhouetted him; it was a fantastic opportunity to capture a simple moment that visually conveyed the most salient aspects of the war fighter. I positioned myself for a side profile as he slowly scanned left and right, and with one of my Canon EOS-1Ds Mark III bodies with an 80–200mm f/2.8 telephoto zoom lens shot a burst of frames. This was the best.

Rocket and Gun Run

Chocolate Mountain Aerial Gunnery Range, California

Close air support, or CAS (pronounced "cass"), ranks among the most dangerous and difficult missions in military aviation. The reasons for its complexities and potential hazards all relate to the first word of the mission, *close*—as in close to friendly ground forces, not close to the ground. Some legendary CAS missions have had jets and helicopters firing upon advancing enemy forces just a dozen or so feet from friendlies, meaning even a slight mishap can end in the wrong people getting hit. The mission requires a tremendous amount of "detailed integration" among those on the ground and those in the air. I photographed this Marine Corps UH-1N Iroquois "Huey" helicopter, armed to the teeth with rockets and guns, practicing CAS at the Chocolate Mountain Aerial Gunnery Range in southern California's Mojave Desert. The live fire gun and rocket runs end with a hard bank and the expenditure of flares—in real world, combat and enemy may take advantage of an aircraft's ingress into their territory and attempt to shoot it down with a surface-to-air missile, which are thwarted by these flares.

I photographed the Huey using a Nikon D300 with a 200–400mm f/4 telephoto zoom lens from atop Observation Point Feets.

Nala

Helmand Province of Afghanistan

I shot this image at a combat outpost, or "COP," called Typhoon-4. The outpost was about a quarter acre in size, hemmed in by a mud wall, and was surrounded by Taliban country. Marines who lived at Typhoon-4 would go months without a proper shower, slept in cramped tents, ate terrible food, and spent a lot of time outside the wire. Military personnel based out of such small COPs lived the most dangerous, most austere existences of anyone in both Iraq and Afghanistan. Comfort at these places was in very short supply, often times non-existent. There were few, if any, moments of "escape time." Ever present danger meant constant vigilance and focus. At Typhoon-4, however, Marines like Richard Laughlin had some moments of reprieve, thanks to Nala the puppy. A patrol had found her abandoned and took her in, despite strict orders to not keep dogs at any outpost. She quickly became an important part of the daily routine. Before Marines would head out on combat operations or patrols—and each knew that because of the danger of the area, it might be his last time—Nala would make the rounds, providing a few seconds of comfort a world away from home.

I kept out of Richard's space by using an 80–200mm f/2.8 zoom lens on one of my Canon EOS-1Ds Mark III bodies to get this photograph of him and Nala.

Ospreys at Night

Camp Bastion, Helmand Province of Afghanistan

I first photographed the Marine Corps MV-22 in the spring of 2005 during the aircraft's operational evaluation (OPE-VAL) phase and was immediately mesmerized by the Osprey. A few years later I embedded with VMM-261, or Marine Medium Tiltrotor Squadron 261, during its deployment to Afghanistan—the very first Osprey unit to deploy to Operation Enduring Freedom. It was a dream project of mine, where I got to sit in the "jump seat" in the Osprey's cockpit as the pilots flew throughout southern Afghanistan during combat support operations. I also flew in the regular passenger hold. During this embed I was able to create a number of images I'd dreamed for years of capturing, like this one, a view of Ospreys spinning up for night-time operations.

I used a Canon EOS-1Ds Mark III with a 24mm f/1.4 lens mounted on a Gitzo carbon fiber tripod and RRS ball head. I kept the camera low to maximize contrast of the Ospreys against the night sky, focused on the foreground Osprey, and made a three minute exposure.

Mike Scholl at Dawn

Hindu Kush of the Kunar Province of Afghanistan

This is my favorite image that I've ever taken, for many reasons. The Marine is Mike Scholl, a Marine Corps machine gunner, and he was twenty-years old in this photograph. I met him just a few weeks prior to this moment, during

my first combat operation. As people tend to do in war zones, we became very good friends very quickly. Mike immediately showed that he was kind, generous, and compassionate, offering me whatever I needed, even if it meant he'd go without. He was that way with everyone. I shot this image of him, holding his M240 machine gun over his shoulder at sunrise, after we'd climbed a steep mountainside out of the Pech River Valley of Afghanistan's Kunar Province. It was a remarkable moment; one that I'll never forget.
I stayed in touch with Mike after that embed, and then met up with him at his home base in Hawaii, and then again as he and his battalion trained for their deployment to Iraq. About a year after I took this photograph of Mike, his wife, Melissa, gave birth to their daughter. Mike was in Iraq at the time, at the beginning of his deployment. He couldn't wait to return home, to meet his daughter in person. That would never happen. A massive IED exploded underneath the Humvee he was manning on the outskirts of the city of Haditha. He clung to life, but ultimately succumbed to his injuries. The date was November 14, 2006. He was twenty-one-years old.

Sprint for Cover!

Helmand Province of Afghanistan

I love this photograph because it makes me laugh—by reminding me of the moment. I was embedded with a squad of Marines in the Helmand Province of Afghanistan when they conducted a surveillance operation. They received fairly reliable intelligence that a regional Taliban leader would be paying a late night visit to a suspected Taliban supporter in the area, and they needed to get "eyes on" to confirm his presence. With an abandoned farm building identified as a potential hide, we moved. But moving involved jumping over deep canals, climbing over mud walls, and then sprinting for cover across open fields. Trying to take pictures, run, and not be near anyone else (called dispersion, so as not to give a potential enemy a bigger target), I had no idea what to do or where exactly to go. The moment shouldn't have been funny—it should have been mortifying—but it was hilarious, and I burst out laughing as I sprinted across this open field. I turned and saw Kory Stone, a machine gunner, sprinting for the next covered position with his heavy M240 machine gun, and instead of continuing to that covered position I decided to capture some images of him. I composed this shot with one of my Canon EOS-1Ds Mark III cameras with an 80–200mm f/2.8 telephoto zoom lens.

Harrier at Sunset

Al Asad Airbase, Al Anbar Province of Iraq

The organic war fighting construct of the Marine Corps is called the Marine Air Ground Task Force, or MAGTF, pronounced "mag-taff." With a MAGTF, all critical components of war fighting capability, from artillery, to logistical support, to tanks, to air power, are woven into one another for the direct support of infantry units. In the wars in Afghanistan and Iraq, the Marine Corps deployed both air ground task forces as well as individual unit types into larger "joint task forces" that consisted of personnel of multiple U.S. Services. With both, Marine Corps aviation, which Marines colloquially call "the Wing," played tremendously important roles in Iraq and Afghanistan. One of the key platforms for Marine aviation—the 'A' in MAGTF—is the AV-8B Harrier II. A ground attack jet, the Harrier can take off and land vertically, so it needs no runway. Harrier pilots performed a number of mission types in Afghanistan and Iraq, including close air support, convoy escort, ISR (intelligence, surveillance, and reconnaissance), as well as some electronic warfare.

After a long embed with a Marine Corps infantry battalion in Iraq, I had the opportunity to photograph some Marine aircraft at Al Asad Airbase. I captured this image of a Harrier as a dust storm approached at sunset with a Nikon F6 film camera and a 70–200mm f/2.8 telephoto zoom lens using Fujichrome Velvia (ISO 100) film.

Out of the Dust Storm

Chocolate Mountain Aerial Gunnery Range, California

The V-22 Osprey is a marvel of modern engineering. The aircraft can take off, land, and hover like a helicopter, but it can speed along in horizontal flight like an airplane, thanks to its rotating engine nacelles (and decades' worth of flight control system development). The business end of the Osprey's propulsion system, its "proprotors" (a portmanteau of propeller and rotor) give the V-22 some interesting operating characteristics. The Osprey's proprotor blades are larger than airplane propellers, but smaller than helicopter rotors—being a fusion of two aircraft types, a fixed-wing airplane and a helicopter, required this. Because of this, however, when flying in helicopter mode, the Osprey's proprotors must spin much faster than a helicopter with a similar maximum takeoff weight to make up the difference. And as anyone who has stood under a hovering Osprey knows, the "rotor wash" comes down like a small tornado (I learned this the hard, very painful way). So in desert environments, during takeoff and landing, Ospreys kick up huge plumes of dust that aviators call "brownouts." I photographed this Marine Corps MV-22 Osprey emerging from a dust storm of its own creation with a Nikon D300 and a 70–200mm f/2.8 telephoto zoom lens during a training exercise at the Chocolate Mountain Aerial Gunnery Range in southern California's Mojave Desert.

War Light

Haditha, Al Anbar Province of Iraq

While I always had "pre-visualized" images in mind during my combat embeds, I also kept constantly vigilant for "images of opportunity" that I hadn't pondered, but I knew could emerge within a fraction of a second. What I also realized with war photography, like other types of photography, is that one should also be on the lookout for "lighting of opportunity." This image, which I photographed during a combat operation in the city of Haditha, Iraq, resulted in such an observation. I followed a squad of Marines as they went room to room in a building, "clearing" each. These were high adrenaline moments, as each time you enter a room things can go really badly really quickly as a result of a booby trap or an ambush. As the heart pounding slowed on entering the room in this image and found nothing but rubble, I immediately recognized a unique lighting situation as the Marine I accompanied made final checks of the space. The bright light coming through the window would silhouette that aspect of him in front of the window, but that light would also be reflected back onto him, illuminating his legs. It was a rare instance of natural fill-lighting, no flash needed. Even better—flash fill would have erased the silhouette and overexposed his legs. It was one of the rarest lighting opportunities I've ever encountered. Acting fast as he walked toward the window, I exposed this shot with a Nikon F6 film camera and a 17-35mm zoom lens and Fujichrome Velvia (ISO 100) film.

In the Highback

Kunar Province of Afghanistan

Some of the most harrowing moments for me covering the wars in Afghanistan and Iraq came during my first embed, while in the back of "highback" Humvees. Highbacks were regular Humvees, with light armor plating around the rear passenger area and steel bench seats. On asphalt or smooth dirt roads, they were fine, but over rutted, bumpy roads, they were downright dangerous. A few times I saw a Marine almost get tossed out by the violent bouncing of the Highback during a high speed convoy. Returning from a small combat operation, I saw how these two Marines, Mario Anes and Rob Williams, were perfectly lit, with an Apache gunship in the background flying cover. This was a difficult shot to get as we were moving fast over a really bumpy road (to avoid IEDs). Using a Nikon F6 film camera with a 17–35mm f/2.8 zoom lens, I did my best to frame the image and fired a sequence of frames of Fujichrome Velvia (ISO 50 film. This one came out. Those are some really tough Marines, and this was their life, day in, and day out.

SAW Around the Corner

Haditha, Al Anbar Province of Iraq

Fear. Anxiety. Trepidation. Anticipation. More fear. I remember all of these emo-

tions rushing through me during combat operations and foot patrols while embedded in Iraq. The most intense moments came when turning a corner or entering a room in an abandoned house. An ambush? An improvised explosive device? A sniper shot to the head? I photographed this SAW (squad automatic weapon) gunner as he slipped around a corner. I was next around the corner and quickly made this image using a Nikon F6 film camera and a 70–200mm f/2.8 telephoto zoom lens and Fujichrome Velvia (ISO 100) film. Keep focused by keeping focused and taking more photographs!

Mountain LZ

Rocky Mountains of Colorado

Helicopter pilots and crew have some of the most dangerous and difficult jobs in the military. This danger increases exponentially when flying at high altitude and in mountainous environments for a host of reasons, including decreased engine and rotor system performance. In Afghanistan, where combat often took place at altitudes in excess of 12,000 feet above sea level, these conditions called for highly specialized skills for the numerous mission types helicopter pilots and crew performed. At the Colorado National Guard's HAATS, or High Altitude Army National Guard Aviation Training Site, located high in the Rocky Mountains, instructor-pilots teach these skills to helicopter pilots of all U.S. military services as well as those of foreign ally nations. Seen here, an Army UH-60 Black Hawk approaches a landing zone, or LZ, at over 11,000 above sea level.

I photographed the Hawk with one of my Canon EOS-1Ds Mark III cameras with at 16–35mm f/2.8 zoom lens.

Focus

Helmand Province of Afghanistan

I've never witnessed "fearlessness" in combat. Military practitioners dismiss the

notion as reckless, despite some popular media myths. What I have witnessed is focus—on every combat operation and patrol that I've joined. Every second of combat is fluid and dynamic, characterized by a host of ever-changing variables that absolutely demand the highest levels of focus. It's exhausting but it keeps the mission in motion.

I photographed this moment of intense focus expressed on the face of Marine SAW (squad automatic weapon) gunner Justin Slagowski during a dangerous operation to find a Taliban commander in Afghanistan's restive Helmand Province. I used one of my Canon EOS-1Ds Mark III cameras with an 80–200mm f/2.8 telephoto zoom lens.

Harriers Over Al Anbar

Over the Al Anbar Province of Iraq

When I first expressed interest in embedding with military units—and was offered the opportunity to actually go "down range"—I never could have imagined in my wildest fantasies some of the places I'd go, nor the sights I'd see, nor the photo shoots I'd do. This is one such unbelievable photo shoot. I call it a C-130 ramp shoot, where I'm tethered to the inside of a C-130, a loadmaster lowers the rear loading ramp, I walk to the very edge of that ramp and look down at thousands of feet of air between my feet and the ground (and yes it's very loud), and then jets fly up and I photograph them. I did five of these ramp shoots in Malaysia during training and two in Iraq, during actual combat. In all of them, the primary mission was to refuel aircraft, but the secondary mission was to allow me to get some incredible photographs. This was my second ramp shoot in Iraq—my first was with a Marine Hornet squadron, and when a Harrier squadron heard about it, they made quick plans for me to photograph them the next morning. Here they are about to break away, loaded with live weapons, roughly two miles over the Al Anbar Province of Iraq.

I photographed them with a Nikon D200 and a 12–24mm f/4.0 lens. I directed them by hand—they were so close at one point (like thirty feet) I had to back them off as my lens couldn't get them both in the frame. Amazing pilots.

Euphrates Patrol

Al Anbar Province of Iraq

Much of my time covering ground combat in Iraq was filled with trepidation and downright fear. A lot of friends I had made died, and as I spent a lot of time outside the relative safety of bases, I risked that eventuality myself. I'm not exaggerating at all when I say that each footstep outside the wire can be the last. There were moments, however, of beauty and fascination. One morning I joined 1st Lieutenant Brian Park on a patrol he led along the Euphrates River. The Euphrates is a corridor rich in history, and on that morning we came upon some ruins. No idea how old, nor who built the original structures, nor what they were, but it was a pleasant escape from the realities of war. Using a Nikon F6 film camera with a 70–200mm f/2.8 telephoto zoom lens, I captured Brian as he walked past an opening, with the Euphrates beyond.

Nose for Explosives

Helmand Province of Afghanistan

Military working dogs, or MWDs, play a number of important support roles for their human counterparts in combat operations. One of the most important during the wars in Afghanistan and Iraq was sniffing out hidden explosives, the job of the dog seen here with his handler. Some military working dogs, however, don't like combat very much and "desert." I met one of these "conscientious canine objectors" at a small, very remote combat outpost. Her name was Lottie, and she never left the wire. The enemy ambushed her unit on her first combat operation, and when her human counterparts fired back, the loud bangs freaked her out and she bolted. So in addition to fighting the enemy, the troops had to track down Lottie. Twelve hours later they found her in a field, curled up trying to sleep. They brought her back to base to make

arrangements to send her home. For some unknown reason, however, she was officially reported missing in action. She hung around and performed the vital job of "testing" summer sausage, Rice Crispy treats (her favorite), and beef jerky.

I shot this photograph with a Canon EOS-1Ds Mark III with a 16–35mm f/2.8 zoom lens.

Rocket Down Range

Near Yuma, Arizona

The helicopter in this photograph is the UH-1N Iroquois, often called the "Twin Huey" or the "November" (Phonetic for "N"). A utility helicopter, hence the U in its name, this aircraft served the U.S. military in a wide range of roles for decades, including assault support, logistics, convoy escort, and close air support, or CAS. For the CAS role, the November could be loaded up with an array of guns and rockets. Seen here, a UH-1N fires a 2.75 inch diameter "Hydra 70" rocket during close air support training.

I shot this photograph with a Nikon D300 and a 70–200mm f/2.8 telephoto zoom lens.

...When You Can Get It

Kandahar Province of Afghanistan

... As in sleep, and for that matter, where you can get it. The father of a friend of mine once told me that in the Army he learned to get "two minutes of sleep at a time." I thought that sounded crazy—until I started embedding. You move when you have to move, stop when you have to stop, and sleep whenever you can get it, even if you're sitting in the back of a troop transport, all "geared up" with a

flak jacket and Kevlar helmet. Or like this guy, waiting for a helicopter.

I shot this photograph with a Canon EOS-1Ds Mark III camera and an 80–200mm f/2.8 telephoto zoom lens.

On the Mark

Outside Marjah, Helmand Province of Afghanistan

When I arrived at my destination base during my first combat embed, I was given a crash course in the use of basic infantry weapons. I also "embedded within my embed" for a few hours with a sniper team. They're highly specialized, and thus there are few of them. In the world of modern combat, however, particularly in Iraq and Afghanistan, the military saw the need for personnel trained as what could best be called a "snipers light." Enter the DM, or designated marksman.

I shot this photograph of a DM during a combat operation near the city of Marjah, in Afghanistan's Helmand Province with a Canon EOS-1Ds Mark III camera body and an 80–200mm f/2.8 telephoto zoom lens as he aims his M39 EMR, enhanced marksman rifle.

Dawn Patrol

Hindu Kush of Afghanistan's Kunar Province

I wrote about Jeremy Sandvick Monroe in the description of the image entitled "SAW Gunner" featured on page 8 of this book. I shot this photograph of Jeremy (foreground) and a fellow Marine just minutes after I shot "SAW Gunner." This image provides a much wider view, showing the steep, rugged—and very beautiful—Hindu Kush over which Jeremy and the Marines of his platoon traveled on a daily (and nightly) basis. The dawn light accentuated the texture of the truculent landscape. The morning light also clearly illuminated Jeremy's look of focused intent on the mission at hand. Jeremy was almost always out in front, "on point," during operations, and he never became even slightly fatigued, despite the oppressively constrictive and heavy flak jacket (with bulky ceramic inserts) and Kevlar helmet he wore, not to mention the weight of everything else he carried.

I shot this image with a Nikon F6 film camera and a 17–35mm f/2.8 zoom lens using Fujichrome Velvia (ISO 50) film. RIP Jeremy.

IED Wire

Al Anbar Province of Iraq

1st Lieutenant Regan Turner grabbed me shortly after I'd arrived at my destination base in Iraq for my first embed

there: "Let's go," he said. "Get all your gear, and let's go. We're headed out in an hour." Of course I said yes, despite lack of sleep in the past few days. Two hours later I was deep in a patrol hunting for any sign of one of the most deadly weapons used in the wars in Afghanistan and Iraq: improvised explosive devices, or IEDs. "Look, " Regan said after showing me a crater of a massive IED that had recently killed and maimed. "Component wire."

I took this image of Regan holding wire that likely was used for an IED just as the sun closed on the western horizon. I used a Nikon F6 film camera and a 70–200mm f/2.8 telephoto zoom lens and Fujichrome Velvia (ISO 100) film.

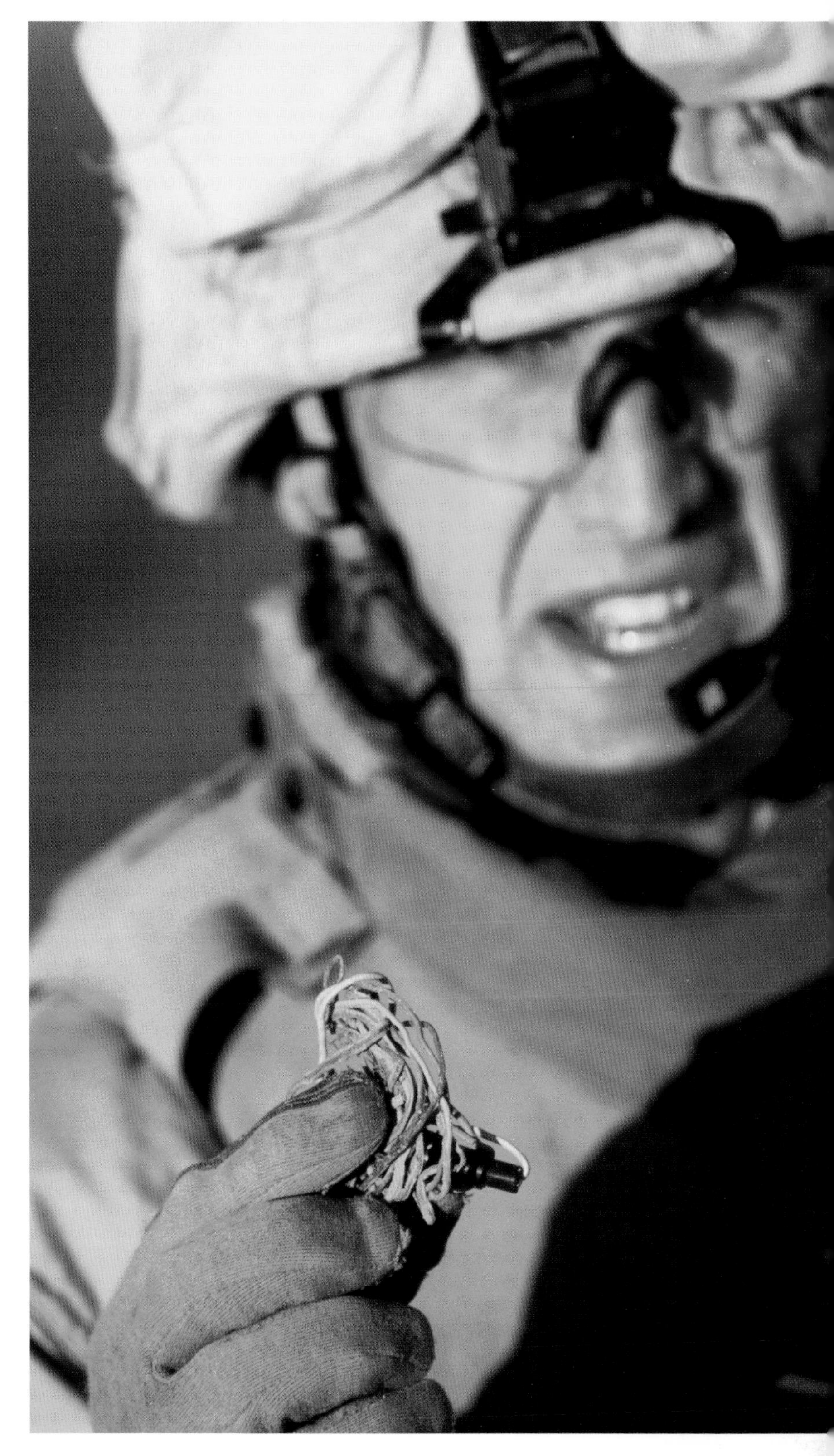

Birds Inbound

Jalalabad, Nangarhar Province of Afghanistan

Troops on the ground love hearing the phrase "birds inbound." It means helicopters are approaching, an in the case of these birds, CH-47 Chinooks, it can mean a resupply during the middle of an operation, a fast insert to start an operation, or an extract at the end of an operation. Due to the high threat of improvised explosive devices in both Afghanistan and Iraq, ground troops almost universally preferred to move around in helicopters over walking or on convoys. Furthermore, pilots and crew of Chinook and other transport helicopter units knew how tough things could get for ground troops, and would often bring them some of their own supplies—notably energy drinks called "Rip Its," chewing tobacco, Gatorade, and beef jerky. "Birds inbound" was a great phrase indeed.

I photographed these Chinooks inbound to an airfield in Jalalabad with a Nikon F5 film camera with a 70–200mm f/2.8 lens and Fujichrome Velvia (ISO 50) film.

Long Shadow of the War Fighter

Helmand Province of Afghanistan

Over the years I've run across a lot of misunderstanding and misconceptions about modern war and the modern war fighter. Regardless of one's opinion about a specific war, a specific operation, or even a specific branch of the military, war changes history. And thus, every member of the military engaged in war fighting casts a long historical shadow (in my opinion). I was at the end of a combat patrol when I saw this scene materialize, and I actually did think, 'wow, the long shadow of the war fighter.' I didn't get too wrapped up and whacked out in metaphor, though—that would be reckless in a combat zone, but I thought hard enough to grab my Canon EOS-1Ds Mark III camera with a 16–35mm f/2.8 lens and compose this shot so I could ponder it further later on down the line.

Hornets at Dusk

Over the Al Anbar Province of Iraq

Designed and built from the start to be both an air-to-air fighter and an air-to-ground attack aircraft, the F/A-18 Hornet played crucial roles in the wars in Afghanistan and Iraq. I photographed these two F/A-18D Hornets during a close air support mission in the Al Anbar Province of Iraq. They were supporting an operation and stayed overhead as long as possible for ground troops, but needed fuel. I was in a Marine Corps KC-130J refueling aircraft, and as the Hornets approached, the loadmaster dropped the rear loading ramp, and, safely tethered, I walked to the edge just as dusk was approaching. The timing was perfect for this silhouette shot.

I photographed them refueling, and then sat down and leaned out with my Nikon D200 with a 50mm f/1.4 lens and click-click-clicked away as they gave me a few seconds of slow drift off the right rear of the tanker before breaking hard and racing back to the fight.

Night View of MRAPs

Helmand Province of Afghanistan

The U.S. military countered the threat of improvised explosive devices (IEDs) in a number of ways. One of the most salient, and important, was the use of MRAPs, or mine-resistant, ambush-protected vehicles. Humvees, even "up armored" Hummers, weren't tough enough to withstand the often massive IEDs insurgents and terrorists would detonate. MRAPS are heavily armored, and are actually comfortable to ride around in.

I photographed these three MRAPs (the two on the left are all terrain versions) at a forward operating base in Afghanistan's Helmand Province. Just after the sun had set, I set up a Canon EOS-1Ds Mark III camera with a 24mm f/1.4 lens on a Gitzo carbon fiber tripod with a RRS ball head. To balance the final glow of twilight in the background, I used a Petzl headlamp (with a halogen bulb, which has a warmer color signature than light emitting diode bulbs) and "painted" the MRAPs with light over the course of the long exposure, which also captured star trails above and—to my surprise—a meteor streak.

A Visit to TRP-12

Hindu Kush of Afghanistan's Kunar Province

The military uses a number of ways to identify points on the ground, and none are very prosaic. One such way is the target reference point, or TRP. This is TRP-12, near the village of Nangalam, in Afghanistan's Kunar Province. It's one of the most beautiful places I've ever visited. My journey to TRP-12 started out with a loud bang, as in 120mm mortars launching toward TRP-12 to "prep" (scare away or kill any Taliban who might cause problems) an LZ (landing zone). Then the Chinook helicopters came with AH-64 Apache gunship escort. And then we all loaded into the "birds" to pay a personal visit to TRP-12. Accompanying the American troops and their weapons and food in the Chinooks were Afghan fighters with their weapons and food—live goats and chickens.

We landed, jumped out, and I went to work photographing the exhilarating moment. I shot this image of a radio operator reporting to higher command that we'd inserted without incident using a Nikon F6 film camera with a 17–35mm f/2.8 zoom lens and Fujichrome Velvia (ISO-50) film. Later that night we all relaxed under the stars and the hum of an AC-130 gunship orbiting overhead and ate some great—and very fresh Afghan cuisine.

Hawg Maintenance

Bagram Airfield

The Air Forces' A-10 Thunderbolt II is a legendary ground attack jet that continued to burnish its classic reputation throughout the wars in Iraq and Afghanistan. Built around the General Electric GAU-8 Avenger 30mm high speed rotary cannon that fires at a rate fires at a rate of roughly 70 rounds per second, the A-10 can carry a number of other weapons including bombs, rockets, and missiles. Despite its official name, Thunderbolt II (it's the namesake of the classic World War II P-47 Thunderbolt fighter/bomber), most know the A-10 as the Warthog, the Hog, or (primarily among A-10 pilots, maintainers, and crew), the Hawg. Unfortunately, the A-10 has a reputation for being ugly. It's not ugly at all, but beautiful and elegant in its strict utilitarianism. And it's definitely not an ugly sight whatsoever to the troops on the ground that the A-10 supports (often with the gun, shooting high explosive rounds).

Here's one I photographed under regularly scheduled "phase" maintenance at Bagram Airfield. I used a Canon EOS-1Ds Mark III camera with a 14mm f/2.8 lens mounted on a Gitzo carbon fiber tripod and a RRS ball head.

Canal Jump

Helmand Province of Afghanistan

Yikes! Does this image bring back memories. Talk to anyone who has spent time outside the wire in Afghanistan's Helmand Province and they'll tell you: don't look at the map and think the flat terrain is easy to traverse—it's crisscrossed with deep (and often wide) canals, and you have to jump many of them to get from one point to another. Bad jumps and worse landings caused lots of sprained ankles, twisted knees, and broken bones. Think your morning commute is tough? Take a look at this Marine. In his left hand he's holding an MK12 SPR (Special Purpose Rifle) that weighs ten pounds (not including ammo). He's wearing oppressively constricting and heavy body armor, and a helmet, and a pack that weighs in excess of fifty pounds, and grenades, and a radio, and more. Just another day in the life.

I photographed this moment with one of my Canon EOS-1Ds Mark III cameras with an 80–200mm f/2.8 telephoto zoom lens.

Into the Big Desert Sky

Al Asad Airbase, Al Anbar Province of Iraq

Photographing aviation assets launching and landing at a large airbase in a war zone kept me busy, particularly during early mornings and late afternoons when lighting is most dramatic. The problem for me was often one of abundance—so many aircraft and photographic possibilities, and so few seconds to choose and then to compose and shoot. I gave up on a shot of an F/A-18 hornet landing to grab this image of an AV-8B Harrier II launching. The Harrier was far enough away that even with my 70–200mm f/2.8 telephoto zoom lens at 200mm using my "crop frame" Nikon D200, it would still render fairly small in the final image. But I made a split decision to "break contact" from the Hornet and go for this shot as it showed, very dramatically with the silhouette, the aircraft roaring into the big desert sky.

Helmet Flag

Hindu Kush of Afghanistan's Kunar Province

The Marine in the foreground of this image is Justin Bradley. I met him at the start of my first embed, in Afghanistan, and we became great friends. He'd heard that a photographer was showing up, and so he sewed this American flag onto the back of his helmet. I spent a lot of time trailing Justin during combat patrols in the Hindu Kush and got a lot of great photographs of him. This is my favorite. I shot it a bit after sunrise, as the light of the sun crept down the mountainside on which he and another Marine patrolled. The American flag was staged, but this moment was not. I captured it with a Nikon F6 film camera and a 17–35mm f/2.8 zoom lens and Fujichrome Velvia (ISO 50) film.

Unrestricted Takeoff

Al Asad Airbase, Al Anbar Province of Iraq

I swear my ears were still ringing a year after I shot this photograph. I was driving around Al Asad Airbase in Iraq's Al Anbar Province with a crew chief for Marine Fighter Attack Squadron (All Weather)-121 (VMFA(AW)-121), the "Green Knights," when this F/A-18D of the squadron lined up to launch. "Wanna get up close?" The crew chief asked. Of course I did. I readied my Nikon D200 with a 70–200mm telephoto zoom lens as he slammed the gas pedal to the floor and we raced to get the shot. He stopped about 30 yards from the runway and I already had the door open as the Hornet rocketed toward us. I hopped out and started sprinting—then I heard the horn of the crew chief's truck blaring. I turned and he was out jumping up and down yelling "you forgot your cranial! Your ears!!" The cranial is a helmet with built in hearing protection. I looked at him. I looked at the approaching jet. I Stopped for a quarter second, and just kept sprinting. I tracked the Hornet through the viewfinder as the pilot pulled the gear up and raced down the runway at close to 400 miles per hour just a few feet above the runway—he was about to perform an "unrestricted climb." I framed the jet in the "low transition" portion of the takeoff and tracked him. I was so close I had to zoom out to keep the entire Hornet in the frame. BOOM! I nailed the shot just as it passed by, I dropped my camera and covered my ears just as the Hornet pulled vertical, rolled, and raced out of sight.

Blessing M2

Nangalam Village, Kunar Province of Afghanistan

This gun in this photograph is a true legend. It's officially called the M2 heavy machine gun, but it goes by a number of different names: "The 50," "The .50 cal," and "Ma Deuce," among others. Designed at the end of the First World War, the M2 is still in use today, and played major roles throughout both the war in Afghanistan and the war in Iraq.

I photographed this 50 at a bunker at Firebase Blessing, outside the village of Nangalam in Afghanistan's Kunar Province. I used a Nikon F6 film camera with a 17–35mm f/2.8 zoom lens, a Nikon Speedlight for fill flash, and Fujichrome Velvia (ISO 50) film.

Overwatch

Al Anbar Province of Iraq

In Iraq, insurgents, terrorists, and snipers hid in palm groves which allowed them to strike without being seen. Every time I got near a palm grove, I double checked my body armor and Kevlar helmet. During one patrol, near the city of Haditha, in Iraq's Al Anbar Province, I shadowed a SAW (squad automatic weapon) gunner. As we approached a palm grove on the edge of a neighborhood torn apart by the war, the gunner took up carefully selected "overwatch" positions as the rest of the squad moved past. Then he'd race ahead, leap frogging the others, and take up another position. If anything happened, he'd open up with ten shot bursts aimed toward the area of activity as the others took cover. I was able to get this photograph of him with a Nikon F6 film camera and a 17–35mm f/2.8 zoom lens and Fujichrome Velvia (ISO 100) film.

Civil Affairs in a War Zone

Haditha, Al Anbar Province of Iraq

This was one of those "images of opportunity." While embedded in the Haditha region of Iraq's Al Anbar Province one late afternoon, I prepared to leave the safety of base for a patrol with a squad of Marines. The light was perfect, but focused on ensuring my helmet and flak jacket was secured just how it should be, I almost missed this image. I took note of the irony of the scene of "Civil Affairs" in a war zone. Civil Affairs is actually a very important job in the Marine Corps in counterinsurgency campaigns, and many Marines performed this job in both Afghanistan and Iraq during the wars there.

With a Nikon F6 film camera and a 70-200mm f/2.8 lens and Fujichrome Velvia (ISO 100) film, I framed this shot, metering an average between the shadowed wall and the front-lit Marine as he passed by.

Vipers of the Mile High Militia

Over the Rocky Mountains of Colorado

In 2011 I was presented with a wonderful opportunity: embed with the 120th Fighter Squadron of the Colorado Air National Guard and interview the pilots and crew about how they train and patrol the air to thwart a 9/11 style attack, should one occur again. The cover story for the September, 2011 issue of Smithsonian's *Air & Space* magazine, I wrote it and also photographed the article, including a flight in a two-seat F-16 to shoot the cover image of two F-16s of the 120th, the "Mile High Militia," pulling vertical over the Rocky Mountains. I briefed for an hour with the three pilots of the "Vipers" (colloquial name for the F-16) on just how we'd pull it off, including studying some computer graphics I drafted to help pre-visualize the shoot. We tried a number of times, and finally nailed it (due to the incredible flying skills of the pilots). On our flight back, I grabbed this image of the two "model" aircraft lit against a distant, darkening storm. I used a Canon EOS-1Ds Mark III camera with a 24–70mm f/2.8 zoom lens for the image.

Airplane Mode Over the Desert

Kandahar Province of Afghanistan

During my embed with Marine Medium Tiltrotor Squadron 261 (VMM-261) during their deployment to Afghanistan, one of my key pre-visualized images was a head-on view of the V-22 Osprey in airplane mode. But not just any head-on shot of an Osprey in airplane mode, I wanted one with the aircraft strongly contrasted against a desert backdrop that showed "sweep" of the proprotors—while keeping the rest of the aircraft tack sharp. No easy feat, especially in the high-vibration environment of another Osprey. One afternoon, after we launched from Kandahar Airfield, I saw the image coming together. I was on the loading ramp of the lead Osprey, squeezed up against a .50 caliber machine gun. With a Canon EOS-1Ds Mark III camera and an 80–200mm f/2.8 telephoto zoom lens, I framed the trailing V-22 in my viewfinder. To ensure "sweep" of the proprotors, I set the metering system for shutter priority, and fixed the shutter speed at 1/125 second. Then both aircraft started banking hard, and climbing. Pressed against the ramp, I fired off shot after shot for a few seconds. This was the best shot, one of my favorites I've ever taken of the Osprey.

Scanning the Distance

Helmand Province of Afghanistan

Canals, mud walls, and open fields—that's what defines much of the Helmand Province of Afghanistan. The canals can prove a nightmare to jump, and the mud walls can conceal Taliban, and then the open fields can be a death trap not only because there's no cover, but because the Taliban often would hide improvised explosive devices on any pathway through them. For all combat operations and patrols, you go from one covered position to the next, as fast as you can move. I shot this photograph using a Canon EOS-1Ds Mark III body with a 16–35mm f/2.8 zoom lens just before we sprinted across the field in the foreground to another covered position. BUT—we all had to use different routes to that next position to stay dispersed (separated to not give an ambusher a bigger target) and to minimize loss should an improvised explosive device explode. I just wanted to keep photographing this Marine scanning the distance. But nope. Time to go. And go like mad we did.

Mobile Combat Operations Center

Helmand Province of Afghanistan

"Distributed ops," or distributed operations, was the name of the game throughout much of the wars in Afghanistan and Iraq. What does "distributed operations" mean? What it doesn't mean is one large mass of troops fighting against another big mass of enemy troops at one well-defined front. To the contrary, distributed ops has smaller units of personnel scattered throughout a large area, each waging its own campaign. That, however, leads to a host of problems concerning what the military calls C2, or command and control. A host of tools enable commanders to maintain solid C2 throughout a distributed ops battlespace, including communications tools, computers, and live video feed from both manned and unmanned aircraft. This image illustrates another tool, the mobile combat operations center. Based in an MRAP (mine resistant, ambush protected) vehicle,

commanders can not only keep tabs on all personnel and events of a distributed ops battlespace, they can pay any of them a visit. I photographed this scene with a Canon EOS-1Ds Mark III camera with a 14mm f/2.8 lens using a Gitzo carbon fiber tripod and a RRS ball head.

Abrams in Repose

Al Anbar Province of Iraq

I've never ridden in (or on) an M1A1 Abrams main battle tank, but during an embed in Iraq, I had the opportunity to climb inside one. It's not for the claustrophobic. Every cubic millimeter of space is used, and there is little room for the four-person crew. The Abrams is armed and armored to the hilt. One of the most important jobs the tank undertook in the Iraq war (the Abrams was used in Afghanistan, but just once, and for a short period of time) was clearing routes for other, less heavily armored vehicles. I shot this photograph of an Abrams with an "M1 Mine Clearing Blade System," also known as a "mine plow" (the claw-like implement at the front of the tank).

For this photograph I used a Nikon F6 film camera and a 70–200mm f/2.8 telephoto zoom lens and Fujichrome Velvia (ISO 100) film.

Maintaining the 240

Helmand Province of Afghanistan

The M240 medium machine gun is a tried and true infantry weapon system. Like all weapons, to work right—or at all—it needs to be maintained to high standards. I photographed Marine machine gunner Jesse Gonzales diligently cleaning and oiling his 240 before he grabbed a few hours of sleep at a tiny and very austere combat outpost in Afghanistan's Helmand Province. A quick note about the 240: if an infantry unit has two or more M240s, they "talk" to each other during a firefight. One gunner will fire a burst, and then that burst is immediately "answered" by a burst from another, and then the conversation continues, back and forth (or among three or more). I first learned about "talking guns" during my first firefight, in Afghanistan. Despite the adrenaline of the moment—with enemy rounds snapping and whizzing above us—it really did sound like a legitimate, Morse code-ish discussion.

Dusk Flight of the Black Hawk

Bagram Airfield, Afghanistan

I've always believed in "the eye above the equipment" and have sought to own and use gear that would never limit my capabilities as a photographer. Every once in a while, however, I happen upon a situation where the gear makes a shot even better than my "eye" could have imagined. This was the case with this image. I was at Bagram Airfield in Afghanistan, and the sun had long set. Thinking that shooting was done for the evening, I noticed a Sikorsky Black Hawk helicopter lift off to the north of me. It was a long way off, so I grabbed my Canon 300mm f/2.8 lens and attached it to one of my EOS-1Ds Mark III camera bodies, making sure to activate the lens's image stabilization function, then I tracked the Black Hawk in my viewfinder. Even with the ISO set at 250, and the lens wide open at f/2.8, there was only enough light for the very slow shutter speed of 1⁄50 of a second. With the shot perfectly balanced to include a comfortable amount of sky and the distant snow capped Hindu Kush, I fired the shutter a few times. The slow shutter speed made for great rotor blur, and my tracking the helicopter blurred the background which gave a desired sense of motion of the helicopter. Due to this incredible lens, however, the helicopter itself was rendered tack sharp.

Nighttime Surveillance

Helmand Province of Afghanistan

I captured this image while embedded with a squad of Marines who were on the hunt for a Taliban leader in Afghanistan's restive Helmand Province. We "set up shop" in an abandoned mud-walled farm building near a home the leader was expected to visit in the middle of the night, and then waited and watched. Restless, I really wanted to create a photograph that illustrated the mission, which is technically called covert surveillance and reconnaissance. BUT—I had to do it in a way that wouldn't reveal our presence, so obviously flash photography was way out of the question. And I couldn't make any noise, and couldn't venture more than a few feet from our hide. I crept outside to see what I could do and noticed SAW (squad automatic weapon) gunner Joey Marshall watching the target house through his night vision goggles. He barely moved as he kept close watch on the house, waiting for the leader to arrive. "Hey Joey," I whispered. "I'm going to take your picture. Stay still just like that." The faint glow from his night vision goggles bobbed slowly up and down in an "OK" gesture. I set up one of my Canon EOS-1Ds Mark III cameras with a 24mm f/1.4 lens on a Gitzo carbon fiber tripod with a RRS ball head and exposed Joey, behind his glowing night vision goggles, for eight minutes.

The FE and Chalk-2

Over the Kunar Province of Afghanistan

CH-47 flight engineers ("FEs") play a number of critical roles as part of a Chinook helicopter crew. They know the "bird" inside and out, and everything about recent maintenance and aircraft performance capabilities. They're also in charge of aircraft cargo—which in a Chinook is complicated business as the aircraft can carry loads inside as well as "slung" off of hooks located on the underside of the CH-47 (Chinook pilots and crew sometimes call themselves "hookers" because of this external load feature). One of the most important roles flight engineers play is crewing the ramp gun during combat operations. If an enemy on the ground starts firing, the ramp gunner (along with the two door gunners) are well trained to accurately fire back. While flying through the Kunar Valley in Afghanistan's Kunar Province, I photographed both the flight crew manning the gun, as well as the Chinook trailing us, called "Chalk 2" in Army aviation parlance (I was in Chalk 1). I used a Nikon F5 film camera and a 70–200mm telephoto zoom lens and Fujichrome Velvia (ISO 50) film, focusing on Chalk 2.

Moon Dust

Jalalabad, Nangarhar Province of Afghanistan

I've never experienced dust quite like that which I witnessed (and breathed in and coughed out) during a convoy from the city of Asadabad, in Afghanistan's Kunar Province, to Jalalabad, in the country's Nangarhar Province. The Marines called it "moon dust" and it was like talcum powder, and there was tons of it. It got onto and into everything, including weapons. I photographed this Marine at the merciful end of the convoy, plastered in moon dust, blowing it off one of his 5.56mm rounds. I used a Nikon F3HP film camera with a 50mm f/1.4 lens and Fujichrome Velvia (ISO 50) film.

Tanks Parking

Haditha, Al Anbar Province of Iraq

While embedded in Afghanistan and Iraq, I'd sometimes forget that I was in a war zone. This didn't happen very often, and when it did happen, it didn't last for more than a few seconds, as I'd get a blunt reminder that indeed, I was in a combat theater. This was one of those blunt reminders. I was in the city of Haditha, in Iraq's Al Anbar Province, visiting an Iraqi police station with some Marines. I didn't need my body armor and helmet, so I took those off (always a bad idea). Walking around with my camera, admiring the sights of that part of the city, I looked up to see "Tanks Parking" spray painted on a chunk of concrete wall, framed by concertina razor wire. Yup, I was in a war zone. I photographed this with a Nikon F6 film camera and a 70–200mm f/2.8 lens and Fujichrome Velvia (ISO 100) film.

Through the Unknown

Kunar Province of Afghanistan

To a farmer, this is a corn field. To U.S. troops who operated in the war in Afghanistan, this is a big thicket of unknown, a place where the Taliban and Al Qaeda would hide and then launch ambushes. Whenever I was with troops heading through a cornfield, I was always prepared to do one thing: jump flat on my stomach and stay as low and close to the ground as possible. One bang and I'd be down. Thankfully, I never heard that bang, so just dutifully moved through the thickets of unknown, and periodically captured the moment with one of my cameras. I created this image with a Nikon F6 film camera

and a 17–35mm f/2.8 zoom lens and Fujichrome Velvia (ISO 50) film.

Idling Echoes

Camp Bastion, Helmand Province of Afghanistan

For many years, the largest and most powerful helicopter in the U.S. Military has been the Sikorsky CH-53E Super Stallion. (Operationally, the Super Stallion, colloquially known as the "Echo" (phonetic for E), retains that title today, although with the introduction of the CH-53K "King Stallion," the Echo will fall to number two). The Echo is a monster. It's maximum takeoff weight is more than triple that of a UH-60 Black Hawk. It's powered by three large turboshaft engines and while it has seating for 55 passengers, it can easily carry twice that many people. They're also impressively loud, both inside and out. Three of them together are absolutely rancorous. I photographed these three idling Echoes at dusk at Camp Bastion, in Afghanistan's Helmand Province with one of my Canon EOS-1Ds Mark III cameras and a 300mm f/2.8 lens.

Turret Gunner

Al Anbar Province of Afghanistan

The turret gunner plays an incredibly important role in any convoy. They are some of the keenest eyes, and very much the first fists to fight in an ambush. The gunner typically mans either a .50 caliber heavy machine gun or an M240 medium machine gun (and sometimes mans two guns: an M240 and a Mk 19 automatic grenade launcher). Prior to the advent of the massive MRAP (mine resistant, ambush protected) vehicles, troops typically used "up-armored" Humvees for convoy operations.

I shot this photograph of a turret gunner from inside the cramped quarters of an up-armored Humvee during a convoy in the Al Anbar Province of Iraq. I used a Nikon F6 film camera and a 17–35mm zoom lens and Fujichrome Velvia (ISO 100) film.

LAR Crew

Helmand Province of Afghanistan

The Canon 300mm f/2.8 lens is a big "super telephoto" optic that photographers often use for wildlife and sports. I brought mine to Afghanistan twice, and despite its size and weight, was always very happy that I had it along. While I used two types of lenses more than any other: a wide angle zoom (16-35mm f/2.8) and a telephoto zoom (70-200 f/2.8), the 300mm proved a go-to for me for many occasions. For war photography, I found the 300mm to be a natural for candid portraiture. The lens's "long reach" allowed me to stealthily capture portraits from a long way off, and it can beautifully isolate subjects with its narrow depth of field (especially when shooting with wide apertures).

I captured this Light Armored Reconnaissance (LAR) crew just before a journey through the desert of the southern reaches of Afghanistan's Helmand Province using the 300 on one of my Canon EOS-1Ds Mark III cameras. One problem with the 300mm: it can prove to be a bullet magnet. It's not a lens that most war photographers carry, and when I ran around with it, those with whom I was embedded would sometimes ask that I put it away—an enemy could mistake me for someone collecting intelligence.

Cockpit of the KC-130J

Over the Kandahar Province of Afghanistan

The military can prove to be a small world. I'd embedded with the two pilots in this photograph during a training exercise in Malaysia, and when I got on board their KC-130J Super Hercules in the Helmand Province of Afghanistan, they recognized me and invited me to join them in the cockpit. It was uneventful, but as we flew into the sun, I recognized the opportunity for a dramatic image. I used one of my Canon EOS-1Ds Mark III cameras and a 16–35mm f/2.8 lens and captured this image of the flight deck with the sun beaming through one of the HUDs, or head-up displays.

Whiskey Cobra

Camp Bastion, Helmand Province of Afghanistan

The AH-1 Cobra is a renowned attack helicopter initially used by the U.S. Army and now used exclusively by the Marine Corps. The iteration of the Cobra used in the wars in Afghanistan and Iraq, the AH-1W SuperCobra, often went by the moniker "Whiskey Cobra" or just "The Whiskey" ("Whiskey" is phonetic for W). Ground troops on combat operations love having low flying attack helicopters like the Army's Apache or the Marine Corps Whiskey overhead. In both Afghanistan and Iraq, the enemy knew to keep fingers off triggers, and to stay well out of sight when Whiskeys were orbiting. They bristle with weapons, and more importantly, the well-trained pilots keep a keen eye for any threats; they are ready to use the aircraft's gun, rockets, or missiles at a second's notice.

I shot this Whiskey at Camp Bastion in Afghanistan's Helmand Province with one of my Canon EOS-1Ds Mark III cameras with a 70–200mm f/2.8 lens.

Inbound to LZ Washington

Baghdad, Iraq

The first part of 2007 was a high threat period in Iraq for American military aircraft of all types, particularly for helicopters. Insurgents and terrorists would often take shots at helicopters with rifles and sometimes with rocket propelled grenades (RPGs). Gunfire and RPGs only hit targets when luck favors the shooter; they're unguided and the vast majority of these shots, in both Afghanistan and Iraq, missed. The big threat in 2007 in Iraq came a type of guided weapon called a MANPADS, or man-portable air-defense system, a jargony term for a shoulder-launched guided anti-aircraft missile. Most MANPADS are of the infrared, or heat-seeking, variety. The American military countered this threat through on-board defense systems that identified an inbound missile and then attempted to confuse its seeker head with high temperature flares. There was another method: while flying over populated areas like Baghdad, go really fast and really low. I was embedded with a Marine Corps CH-46E "Sea Knight" helicopter (colloquially known as a "Phrog") squadron for a couple days in May of 2007. We flew throughout Baghdad and western Iraq, and when over Baghdad, we did indeed fly very low and very fast.

I shot this image from the ramp of the lead ship as we arrived at "LZ Washington" within the Green Zone of Baghdad with a Nikon D200 and a 70–200mm telephoto zoom lens.

High Speed Desert Scan

Helmand Province of Afghanistan

I shot this image from the back of a logistics variant of an LAV-25, a light armored vehicle used by Light Armored Reconnaissance units in the Marine Corps. We were speeding along the open desert of the southern reaches of Afghanistan's Helmand Province, joking about hoping to not hit an improvised explosive device, and this photo opportunity came up when Rick Crevier took a look ahead through the optics on his M4.

I braced myself with my left hand and held one of my Canon EOS-1Ds Mark III cameras with a 16–35mm f/2.8 lens with my right, and clicked away, careful to keep the horizon level (one of my pet peeves—a horizon skewed even a half a degree off is noticeable). We never hit any IEDs, thankfully.

Complacency Kills

Al Anbar Province of Iraq

Complacency kills: Stay alert, stay alive. That”s a phrase I heard over and over again while embedded with troops during training to go to Iraq, and then I heard it even more frequently once I was with troops in Iraq. Of course, sometimes no amount of vigilance can keep a sniper's bullet from striking or stop an improvised explosive device from detonating, but I've heard story after story about how a hyper-alert “sixth sense” saved the day. I photographed this Marine passing the message at a small, frequently-attacked combat outpost in Iraq's Al Anbar Province with a Nikon F6 film camera and a 17–35mm f/2.8 lens and Fujichrome Velvia (ISO 100) film.

The Skinny Ones Shoot Back

Near Yuma, Arizona

A Marine Corps AH-1W "Whiskey" SuperCobra pilot once told me a story about how a captured member of Al Qaeda explained how he and other insurgents would never shoot at Cobra attack helicopters because "the skinny ones shoot back." While that's certainly true, wider, "fatter," transport helicopters are also armed. But they are armed with defensive weapons. The Whiskey is an offensive machine and boasts a powerful 20mm gun under its nose and can carry an assortment of rockets and missiles. I photographed this Whiskey firing a 2.75-inch diameter Hydra 70 rocket during a close air support training exercise. I photographed it using a Nikon D300 and a 70–200mm f/2.8 lens from a point roughly 300 meters from its target.

Infil Complete

Hindu Kush of Afghanistan's Kunar Province

The pilots of these two U.S. Army CH-47D Chinook helicopters flawlessly landed side-by-side during an "infil" (short for "infiltration," which is a term that is interchangeable for "insert") that kicked off a combat operation in the Hindu Kush of Afghanistan's Kunar Province. As a Navy Hospital Corpsman, a medic, kept an eye out for any possible ambushers, the first of the two lifted back into the sky just minutes later after all personnel and cargo was offloaded. Afghanistan's Hindu Kush is a sort of home away from home for the powerful Chinook, in that the helicopter is renowned as a great high altitude performer. I shot this image with a Nikon F6 film camera and a 17–35mm zoom lens and Fujichrome Velvia (ISO 50) film.

Oscar Mike: On the Move

Kunar Province of Afghanistan

"Oscar Mike" phonetically represent the letters O M, which are the key component words to the short phrase: "on the move." Oscar mike is both declaratory: "we're Oscar Mike," as in "we're moving" and motivational, as in "let's be Oscar Mike in less than five." I quickly learned that if you're not inside the security of a base, or in a covered position when outside the wire, the safest way to be is Oscar Mike—harder to an enemy to hit you when you're moving. I photographed these Marines, Oscar Mike, after a successful weapons cache raid in an isolated village near the border between the Kunar Province and the Nuristan Province. I used a Nikon F6 film camera with a 17–35mm f/2.8 zoom lens and Fujichrome Velvia (ISO 50) film.

Dustoff Spinup

Al Asad Airbase, Al Anbar Province of Iraq

U.S. Army UH-60 Black Hawk Air Ambulance MEDEVAC (medical evacuation) pilots and crew perform arguably the most dangerous aviation mission throughout the military: they rescue the injured, and when I say "the injured," I mean American personnel, coalition personnel, civilian personnel, and insurgent and terrorist personnel. They fly with the call sign "Dustoff," which traces its origins to the Vietnam War, and they have undertaken missions in the most dangerous reaches of the wars in Afghanistan and Iraq. Time after time, Dustoffs flew in to active firefights, picked up the injured, and saved lives with just minutes to spare. I embedded with a Dustoff unit for a few nights in Iraq. We flew low and fast all around the country. I photographed this Dustoff "bird" spinning up to head out for a mission with a Nikon D200 camera body and a 12–24mm f/4.0 zoom lens.

Combat Camera

Helmand Province of Afghanistan

I was very fortunate as a combat embed in that the military sent me to some really far flung corners of the wars where they typically didn't let media into. They

weren't kept away for any nefarious reason, but they were kept out of many places I visited simply due to the austerity of these locations. I enjoyed the austerity, and seeing the very front lines. Because of this, many of the images used by media outlets originated from the military itself, in the form of "combat camera" personnel. I photographed this combat cameraman in the Helmand Province of Iraq during a large operation. I used one of my Canon EOS-1Ds Mark III cameras with a 70–200mm f/2.8 zoom lens for the shot. You can also see that he's carrying an M-16 service rifle. There often came times for these photographers to quit one type of shooting, and start another.

Point-to-Point

Al Anbar Province of Iraq

"Don't kick that!" a Marine yelled at me during this patrol. It was just a tube of caulk laying on the ground. "All of this trash can be booby trapped!" He said, referring to improvised explosive devices (IEDs), which were hidden in roads, on trails, in fields, and in walls throughout both Afghanistan and Iraq. When I was on the ground in Iraq, I had two goals: take as many great photographs as possible, and stay alive with all my limbs in place—and I'm not being dramatic about the latter point. While this was never articulated to me in terms of survival, I adopted the "point-to-point" mentality, meaning get from one point of safety to the next as quickly as possible, and try to stay moving as much as possible. I love this image because it really illustrates the point-to-point outlook vividly. I shot it with a Nikon F6 film camera and a 17–35mm f/2.8 lens and Fujichrome Velvia (ISO 100).

The Welcoming Committee

Marjah, Helmand Province of Afghanistan

During combat operations in cities, in both Afghanistan and Iraq, children would often swarm out and greet members of units in which I was embedded. Sometimes they'd ask for candy, sometimes they'd stare, sometimes they'd laugh, sometimes they'd ask for money, and sometimes they'd want to talk about American culture. Once an eight-or-nine-year-old boy just flipped all of us off, but laughed while he was flipping us off. You never knew what was going to happen when children swarmed us, but it was never bad. There always seemed to be laughter, at least by one or two.

I photographed this scene of that city bloc's welcoming committee with one of my Canon EOS-1Ds Mark III cameras and a 16–35mm f/2.8 zoom lens.

Tank Patrol

Haqlaniyah, Al Anbar Province of Iraq

This was the one and only time I went on a combat patrol that included tanks. It seemed like overkill to me to have this massive Abrams tanks rolling down these narrow city streets of Haqlaniyah, in Iraq's Al Anbar Province, but there they were. I watched and photographed as the tanks passed by children and their parents. Some ignored them (hard to do), and some laughed and waved. I shot this image near the beginning of the patrol, using a Nikon F6 film camera and a 70–200mm f/2.8 lens and Fujichrome Velvia (ISO 100) film. A few hours later I got down low at a street corner near an improvised explosive device crater, and with a 17–35mm zoom lens, started shooting some up-close, wide angle shots of the passing tanks. As the second started passing me by, it suddenly accelerated. "Get back!" I heard—I jumped away. The two tanks raced away up a hill. About a half mile away a woman had entered a busy market, walked up to some Marines talking with some of the locals, and then detonated a massive suicide bomb. The tanks sped over to help. It was a long walk back to base.

Yankee Launch

Helmand Province of Afghanistan

The UH-1Y is the latest iteration of the historic Bell UH-1 "Iroquois" helicopter, which became far more commonly known as the "Huey." First introduced in 1959, the Huey became a true legend during the Vietnam War. It continued to prove its utility as both a troop transporter and as a gunship with the UH-1N "November" model in the wars in Afghanistan and Iraq. I photographed this UH-1Y, officially known as the "Venom" but colloquially called the "Yankee," during a large combat operation in the Helmand Province of Afghanistan. The pilots of the helicopter landed in a field to insert some ground troops, and then I got down low on the ground as it lifted back into the sky.

I used one of my Canon EOS-1Ds Mark III cameras with a 16–35mm zoom lens for the shot. There's a bit of history to this shot as this was during the very first combat deployment of the UH-1Y, in 2011.

Nighttime Phrog Maintenance

Al-Taqaddum Air Base, Al Anbar Province of Iraq

While embedded with a Marine Corps CH-46E "Sea Knight" (colloquially the "Phrog") squadron, based out of Al-Taqaddum Air Base in Iraq, I had the opportunity to photograph some of the nighttime maintenance of the helicopters. This was one of my favorites—an image of some maintainers working on the forward rotor hub of the relatively small Phrog. The CH-46 is often confused with the much larger, much more powerful CH-47 Chinook.

I used a tripod-mounted Nikon D200 with a 50mm f/1.4 lens for this 30 second exposure.

Mike, Oscar Mike

Kunar Province of Afghanistan

I wrote about Mike Scholl in the caption for the image *Mike Scholl at Dawn* on pages 64–65. I shot this image just seconds before that one. This was Mike, at his best, under a punishing load, Oscar Mike *(on the move, see page 117)* in the Hindu Kush of Afghanistan's Kunar Province, just as dawn cracked the day open and flooded the mountains with golden light. What an amazing moment. What a great friend. We all miss you.

Index